HOLY SHIFT

LAUGH YOUR MASS OFF

PRAISE FOR HOLY SHIFT

Jonathan Herron is a pastor's kid who was trained in improv by Tina Fey, a life-long church attender who partied with Chris Farley, and now a pastor, who is just the person to teach you how to use comedy in your church to help it fulfill God's mission.

>Vince Antonucci (@vinceantonucci),
>Founding Pastor of Verve Church in Las Vegas, Nevada,
>and author of *Renegade*

I literally could not put this book down which quickly led to two things: 1) I vowed to never attempt to fix something with Crazy Glue before picking up a book to read. 2) As soon as I get this book unstuck from my hands, I'm calling every church pastor I know and telling them this book will revolutionize how they view growing their ministry in a fun and humorous way. Herron perfectly lays out how to put fun, laughter and teamwork back into a church ministry!

>Bob Smiley (@bobsmileycomic),
>comedian and male model (well, not that last one)

I have admired Jon's ability to lead others with a huge smile, an infectious laugh, and a witty sense of humor - even when circumstances got rough. Jonathan's approach to leadership is both refreshing and courageous.

>Scott Thomas (@scottythom),
>Founder of Gospel Coach;
>past President of Acts 29 Network

Growing up in church, I didn't laugh all that much. Maybe at the big hair or the funny deacon, but never during the sermons. Those weren't meant to be entertaining. And that's a shame, because while church isn't entertainment, there's no rule that says it can't be entertaining. That's why I'm glad Jonathan has written this book. It will help bring much-needed laughter to church leaders, which will open doors of ministry to the community. The church is too serious and too important not to learn how to leverage comedy.

> Michael Lukaszewski (@mlukaszewski),
> CEO of Church Fuel and author of *Streamline*

In a day when bookshelves are filled with leadership books repeating the same old ideas, Holy Shift comes along and teaches us new principles in a fresh way. Using great stories as his backdrop, Jonathan leads us on a journey and reminds us how leadership can be fun again. You'll be inspired as you read this book. Plus, you may learn a new joke or two.

> Bob Franquiz (@bobfranquiz),
> Senior Pastor of Calvary Fellowship in Miami, Florida
> and Founder of Church Ninja

Jonathan Herron is an innovative leader, whose life experiences and fresh insights will cause you to laugh, reflect and look at your leadership from a whole new perspective. Holy Shift will cause you to smile, cry and lift you to a higher purpose for developing your leadership gifts.

> Gary P. Rohrmayer (@garyrohrmayer),
> President of Converge MidAmerica;
> co-author of *Church Planting Landmines* and
> *First Steps for Planting a Missional Church*

As a pastor, I know that there's a great deal we can learn from the world of improv. Successful improv artists must collaborate with teams, make split-second decisions, engage groups of people with varied levels of interest, and communicate new thoughts and abstract ideas in meaningful ways; all the while making it look relatively effortless. These are all skills that would greatly benefit any pastor. I'm so glad Jon has written this book and shared some of the insights and secrets he's learned from his amazing improv training and experience.

> Tony McCollum (@tonymccollum),
> Lead Pastor of Fusion Church in Buford, Georgia

Jon Herron brings his unique gift combination of leadership and comedy which provides the church with practical tools for our time. God used him in saving my ministry, and I'm honored to call him a friend and a brother. Read and become a more effective fisher of men.

> Joshua Allen (@joshua_w_allen),
> Executive Pastor of Western Reserve Grace Church
> in Macedonia, Ohio

Jon is a great communicator with a knack of knowing how to jiggle the funny bone. He skillfully uses humor to unfold arms and present the wisdom and truth of the Bible. Despite facing challenging circumstances, Jon has exhibited a calmness that to me has projected a very strong faith.

> Norm Byers (@normbyers),
> Director of Converge Michigan Church Planting;
> Pastor of Genesis Church in Petoskey, Michigan

HOLY SHIFT

JONATHAN HERRON

Foreword by Perry Noble

Holy Shift: Laugh Your Mass Off
Copyright © 2020 Jonathan Herron

All rights reserved. No part of this publication may be reproduced, distributed, or transmitted in any form or by any means, without prior written permission.

Scripture quotations marked (ESV) are taken from The ESV® Bible (The Holy Bible, English Standard Version®) copyright © 2001 by Crossway, a publishing minis-try of Good News Publishers. ESV® Text Edition: 2011. The ESV® text has been reproduced in cooperation with and by permission of Good News Publishers.
Unauthorized reproduction of this publication is prohibited. Used by permission.
All rights reserved.

Scripture quotations marked (KJV) are taken from the King James Bible. Accessed on Bible Gateway at www.BibleGateway.com.

Scripture quotations marked (NASB) are taken from the New American Standard Bible® (NASB), copyright © 1960, 1962, 1963, 1968, 1971, 1972, 1973, 1975, 1977, 1995 by The Lockman Foundation, www.Lockman.org. Used by permission.

Scripture quotations marked (NIV) are taken from the Holy Bible, New International Version. Copyright © 1973, 1978, 1984, 2011 by Biblica, Inc.® Used by permission. All rights reserved worldwide.

Scripture quotations marked (NKJV) are taken from the New King James Version®. Copyright © 1982 by Thomas Nelson, Inc. Used by permission. All rights reserved.

Scripture quotations marked (NLT) are taken from the Holy Bible, New Living Translation, copyright © 1996, 2004, 2015 by Tyndale House Foundation. Used by permission of Tyndale House Publishers, Inc., Carol Stream, Illinois 60188. All rights reserved.

Scripture quotations marked (NRSV) are taken from the New Revised Standard Version Bible, copyright © 1989 the Division of Christian Education of the National

Scripture quotations taken from the Amplified® Bible (AMP), Copyright © 2015 by The Lockman Foundation Used by permission. www.Lockman.org

Second Edition: 2020
Holy Shift / Jonathan Herron
Paperback ISBN: 978-1-951304-17-1

TO MY PARENTS
WHO ALWAYS SAID YES, AND.

When I said I wanted to go into comedy, you said,
"Yes, And let us cheer for you!"

When I said I was enrolling in seminary, you said,
"Yes, And here's a new Bible!"

When I said I was writing a book, you said,
"Will people be able to buy it in a real bookstore?"

You have given me the best gift parents can give:
no boundaries and unconditional belief in their kid's dreams.

TABLE OF CONTENTS

SECTION ONE:
THINK FUNNY 17

1. Did You Hear the One About the Comedian Who Went to Seminary?........................19
2. What if Tommy Boy Led a Church?..................31
3. Humor over Hammer..36

SECTION TWO:
GRAB THE MIC 43

4. Start with a Yes... 45
5. Think Ensemble..68
6. Fail Harder...98
7. Be Completely Unafraid to Die......................112

SECTION THREE:
ACCELERATE CHURCH GROWTH 121

8. Comedy-Driven Sermons................................123
9. Less Cathedral, More Comedy Club.............147
10. How to Handle the Critics..............................156
11. Be You..181

FOREWORD

One of the biggest problems in leadership is that we tend to be way too serious, when, at times, what we all need is a really good laugh.

I remember years ago being in a pretty intense meeting with several staff members as we were trying to solve a problem. The longer the meeting went on the shorter tempers became and, before I knew it, we were all talking about peripheral things that actually had nothing to do with why the meeting had been called in the first place.

It was during that time I had an idea that literally changed the chemistry in the room . . .

I announced the meeting was over and that we were getting into our cars and going bowling.

Everyone looked at me like I had been smoking crack.

"Bowling," I am sure they wondered, "how in the world can we go and bowl at a time like this?"

There was a tad of resistance to the idea; however, I was persistent and we went off to the bowling alley.

And as we were there something amazing happened . . . we began laughing together. For the next two hours we were not focused on solving a problem but rather building community around a fun, common experience.

At this point in the story I wish I could tell you that during the bowling trip someone thought of the solution to the problem, but it would not be true. However, what I can tell you is that the next day, when we gathered in the meeting room to begin to dig into the problem that had so patiently waited on us as we had gone on our bowling endeavor, everyone in the room was way more relaxed and we were able to focus on the issue that needed to be dealt with.

All because we took the time to laugh together.

(And, to be honest, I don't actually remember what the problem was we were trying to solve, but I do remember the bowling trip.)

I am so proud of Jonathan and so thankful he has written this book to guide us all through some things our teams could all use a lot more of . . . laughter.

When people laugh together they are way more likely to work together in harmony.

This is not just a book to be read but rather a guide to help our teams become more functional. I know you will enjoy reading it, and will have a lot of fun along the way.

> Perry Noble
> Founding Pastor of NewSpring Church;
> Bestselling author of *Unleash* and *Overwhelmed*

SECTION ONE

THINK FUNNY

1

DID YOU HEAR THE ONE ABOUT THE COMEDIAN WHO WENT TO SEMINARY?

"You can't be that kid standing at the top of the waterslide, overthinking it. You have to go down the chute." - Tina Fey

Yes, it is true: I partied with Chris Farley two nights before he died.

Ok, now that we've gotten that out of the way, allow me to explain what led to that night in December of 1997, and how it catapulted me into writing this book over fifteen years later.

Go back with me to the late 1970s and early 1980s. A time of childhood innocence, Saturday morning cartoons, and Flintstones vitamins. I grew up in the world of church. Now please don't let that scare you off from reading this book! Whether you go to church or not, the Rules of Comedy will apply in any organization or leadership structure. You just need to know that I'm showing my cards early and coming at things with a rich spiritual history and strong personal belief in God.

My dad was a pastor, which means our family went to church every single Sunday. This was great for introducing me to the gospel and receiving Christ into my life at a young age but was horrible for my chosen vocation of comedy.

You see, we were Presbyterians, a group of Christians not really known for producing high-quality, razor-wit comedians. Our pastors know how to dress up in dark robes like Obi-Wan Kenobi, but we tend to shy away from open-mic comedy nights. Presbyterians must think it's funny to say that we are God's "frozen chosen." I don't get it.

I always found it curious that if you rearrange the letters in Presbyterians, it spells out Britney Spears. That I do get.

Anyhow, I loved our little country church in the fields of Iowa. Looking back now, I realize we didn't have much to do in Iowa. When you're surrounded by cows, chickens, and pigs, your options tend to be limited. In my spare time, I excelled at corn-on-the-cob speed eating. What can I say? We are Iowans. We like simple. We thought that the capital of Wisconsin was W.

Sunday School was fun because the flannel boards were like TV comedies without the laugh track. I provided commentaries out loud and drove the teachers nuts: Why were all the little Bible men wearing dresses? What was up with the sheep being everywhere? Throwing a piglet over your shoulder—that I could understand. But a lamb? And didn't anybody shave back then?

One time before class I drew MC Hammer pants onto little baby Jesus.

Did you know you can actually be expelled from Sunday School?

By the time I got to high school, I had completely tuned out. Bell choir wasn't doing it for me, and our church youth group's idea of a good time was bowling once a month. I loved Jesus but thought church life was like having a spinning hamster wheel but the hamster's dead.

HEY, HEY! WE'RE THE MONKEES!

> *"An art form without an author, improv comedy is sometimes compared to a high-wire act, but truly to understand the level of difficulty, imagine a team of tightrope walkers chained together. Then every few seconds one daredevil must make a sudden, dramatic move."* - The New York Times[1]

Faith was foundational in my life, but it was not my first calling. From a young age, I had always wanted to go into comedy. The idea of making people forget their troubles for a while through laughter appealed to me. The first comedians who truly made me laugh were The Monkees. In 1986, MTV famously ran a random weekend marathon of their popular 1960's TV show. It later provided a platform for a successful 20th anniversary reunion that included a new album, a new Top 20 Hit, and 1987's top-grossing concert tour.

I happened to be at my uncle's house on that fateful weekend in 1986, which was providential since we did not have cable television in my home, but my hip uncle did. As my parents were racing out the door for an appointment, my mom turned on the TV to provide a distraction for me and—boom!—I was introduced to The Monkees. Sure the music was cool, but I was more surprised to see funny grown-ups going on wacky adventures.

A few months later, The Monkees re-appeared on Disney World's 15th Anniversary TV special. I had originally tuned in to watch little Emmanuel Lewis tap-dancing in front of Cinderella's Castle, but was quickly engrossed by the comedy bits starring Micky, Davy, and Peter. I taped it on our brand new, high-tech, cutting-edge VCR and wore out that poor VHS tape watching it over and over again. I was really into The Monkees. During recess on our elementary school playground, I even convinced all my third grade buddies to pretend to be The Monkees. (I was always Micky.)

Always keeping my eye out for these guys that made me laugh so hard, I was rewarded in November of 1987 when The Monkees guest-hosted Nickelodeon's must-see, not-quite-MTV-but-safe-for-elementary-eyes *Nick Rocks* (it was on right after *Danger Mouse* and before *You Can't Do That on Television*). I was hooked.

Ten years later, I took my high school sweetheart on a romantic date to see The Monkees live on tour. It was a blast. Well, for me it was a blast. I think she was just tolerating my crazy little obsession. But two years later, she married me, so its all good in the hood.

Four more Monkees concerts followed in the years ahead. In November of 2012, Micky Dolenz even tweeted out a link to my blog, which absolutely made my year. To say I'm a fan is an understatement. In a sense, they changed my life. Sorta. You see, they influenced me in three key ways:

1. With the exception of Martin & Lewis in 1950, The Monkees program was the first to create television music and comedy through improvisation.

    Yes, they had a script, but the NBC of the late 1960's was sharp and edgy enough to air the improvised bits created on the fly by the boys. Micky, Davy, Mike, and Peter were trained in improv-comedy by James Frowley, a veteran of Second City. When I learned about this connection, I set my heart on learning the Rules of Comedy at the venerable Chicago institution.

2. The theme of the TV series was that they were perpetual underdogs. They never got their big break on the TV show, just shlepping from one gig to another (along with the occasional haunted mansion).

   Perseverance while keeping your sense of humor were the keys to the on-screen band. And guess what? It's true for real world leaders also.

3. The band always had second chances. Their 1987 reunion was the highest-grossing concert tour in the world, their 1996 reunion album received great reviews, and their 2011, 2013, and 2016 reunion tours featured rave reviews from *Rolling Stone Magazine*.

   Even though they were always getting written-off by critics, The Monkees would manage to push forward over the years and keep the fun rolling. I believe this can be true for leaders, too.

The Monkees focused my attention toward comedy while television shows like *SCTV* and *Saturday Night Live* painted a picture of what my future could look like.

As I began studying the biographies of current and past comedians, one theater kept appearing in everyone's bio: The Second City in Chicago.

MY GRADUATION GIFT

"There was something in me that was like, 'I want to do that. I know I can do that.' For some reason it was less scary to me than having words in front of me, because I think when you're handed a script you know that you're supposed to do it in a certain way, and people will think, 'How is she reading this?' But when you're improvising, there's nothing to compare it to and you can do whatever." - Kristen Wiig[2]

The day after I graduated from high school, I begged and pleaded with my parents to drive me to Chicago to see a show at Second City. Somehow my girlfriend (and future wife) and I convinced my parents to drive three hours to 1616 North Wells in the Old Town district of Chicago for the Monday night performance. It was my high school graduation gift from my parents.

The birthplace of improvisational comedy, The Second City in Chicago has produced most of the major comedy stars over the past half century: Alan Arkin, Bill Murray, Gilda Radner, Mike Myers, Stephen Colbert, Steve Carrell, and the voice of Homer Simpson, Dan Castellaneta. Without Second City, there would have been no *Saturday Night Live*, no *Ghostbusters*, no *Late Show with Stephen Colbert*, and no *Simpsons*. If I wanted to move toward writing and performing comedy, Second City was my first stop.

When Second City opened its doors on a snowy Chicago night in December of 1959, no one could have guessed that this tiny Old Town locale would become the most influential and prolific comedy mecca in the world. This theatre tucked in the heart of the Windy City became internationally known for its ever-increasing roster of comedy superstars.

As we parked the car next to a Walgreens a block away from the comedy theater, we looked over our shoulders and noticed another historic landmark: the Moody Church. Constructed in 1924, Moody Church was the result of the aggressive evangelism of Dwight L. Moody in the late 1800's.

Moody was a simple, poorly-educated shoe salesman who felt God calling him to preach. Early one morning he and some friends gathered in a hayfield for a season of prayer, confession, and consecration. Moody's friend, Henry Varley, uttered some challenging words that would forever shape the trajectory of Moody's life: "The world has yet to see what God can do with and for and through and in a man who is fully and wholly consecrated to Him."

Standing on the strength of these words, D.L. Moody courageously moved forward into ministry, leaving the Moody Church in his wake. Beyond the church, Moody also founded what later became Moody Bible Institute, training thousands of Christian leaders for worldwide impact. Reaching over 1,000 children and adults through a new system which Moody coined "Sunday School," Moody's legacy has resulted in a legendary church that sits a mere two blocks away from Second City.

Literally and figuratively, I believe that the intersection of church and comedy can be felt at the corner of North and Wells. Many Second City performers and students (including myself years later) would attend worship at Moody Church on Sundays at 5pm and then head over two blocks to the theater to create comedy. There's a symbiotic relationship there; comedy and leadership are not as far apart as you would suspect.

Fresh out of high school, I found the comedy show that evening to be hypnotic and mesmerizing. I was hooked: Second City was where

I wanted to go and learn the principles of comedy. As soon as I could afford a full tank of gas later that summer, my aim was to wave goodbye to Iowa and hello to Chicago.

Turns out I needed to arrive in the Windy City a few days ahead of Columbia College's freshmen move-in so that I could interview at Second City for a hosting job. When I got the call a few days later that I was hired, I hit the roof! I was in! I didn't care if there was grunt work involved and all my weekend hours would be spent cooking and cleaning; the idea of rubbing shoulders with established comedians was intoxicating.

I went to college full-time, worked 30 hours a week at the theater, and auditioned for the Second City Conservatory Program. After completing Level 1, I met my Level 1A teacher, a main stage writer and actress named Tina Fey. She was gentle and a bit shy but unapologetic about drilling the Rules of Comedy into our impressionable minds. It was like drinking from a fire hose: everything Tina Fey taught me I meticulously recorded and practiced.

A year into my hosting gig at Second City, I had the job down flat. A long line of waiting customers would be busting the door, presenting their tickets to the house manager, who would direct the chaos by handing parties off to each host for seating.

One particularly busy night in the fall of 1997, I was handed the tickets for a couple who were eager for the evening's performance. I quickly sized them up and was astonished at the sight. The young woman was *HAWT* (yes, H - A - W - T)! She was beautiful, blonde, in a gorgeous evening dress, and had sparkling blue eyes. *Hawt.*

Her date, on the other hand, was *NAWT!* He was overweight and sweaty, sported slicked-back-yet-frazzled hair, tie askew... definitely

NAWT! Do you remember the old musical segment on *Sesame Street*: "One of these things is not like the other?" That was this guy! He did NOT go with HER! As I began leading them to their table, I silently wondered, *What is this, a joke? Did she lose a bet somewhere? Is this guy her cousin?*

Their tickets were for the best seats in the house—remarkable because only Second City alumni or relatives and close friends can secure the best seats. I glanced back at the couple to see if I recognized either of them. Nope. Must be friends of a cast member, I guessed.

As I politely pulled back their chairs to help seat them, I looked down at the tickets one last time to quickly use the last name listed and wish them a good evening. They were sitting down as I realized what I was saying mid-sentence: "Thank you for being our guests tonight at Second City, Mr. Faaaaaaaarrrrrrrrley." My mouth went dry as cotton balls and my palms became clammy. This was Chris Farley!

Being a young, impressionable college kid, I felt like I had just hit the jackpot. I had rubbed shoulders with the star of *Saturday Night Live* and *Tommy Boy*, Mr. Living-In-A-Van-Down-By-The-River Himself!

As I stumbled back toward my manager to assist the next guests waiting in line, she grabbed my ear. "You see Mr. Farley over there with his date? We want to make sure he has a very good time tonight. At intermission, I don't want anyone bugging him for photos or autographs. It's going to be YOUR job to usher Farley out of the room and act as his bodyguard."

Bodyguard? Me? Hadn't my manager seen my body frame? If I were a superhero, my name would be Captain Toothpick. In high school football, I didn't just sit on the bench, I lived there. My only secret weapon was that a lean frame made me quick like a ninja. On a few plays, the quarterback would hand me the ball and yell, "Run, Forrest, Run!" I'd oblige with, "Okay, Jen-nay." And boom, touchdown!

At intermission, I dutifully whisked Chris Farley out of the main theater and into a holding room. He was very kind, down-to-earth, and, well, sweaty. But I didn't mind; I had a front-row seat to a rich and famous comedian! We exchanged some small talk, and at the end of the night I thought that was that.

Turns out Mr. Farley would be making multiple visits to the theater over the coming weeks . . . and I was the Tommy Boy star's designated body man for each visit. Over time I was able to closely observe the side effects of stardom.

I remember one night Farley came barreling into the theater with a group of friends. Once we had them seated at a large table near the front, Farley pulled out a wad of hundred dollar bills and began liberally handing them out to his party. They pocketed their cash and scattered. I thought it was odd.

Another time Chris came to a show under the influence of something. He looked like more of a mess than usual and smelled like he hadn't showered in days. When he began loudly heckling the comedians on stage, I had the awkward duty of discreetly trying to remove Chris Farley from the audience.

Even though I was a front-row witness to some blaring warning signs, I had zero sway over Farley's downward spiral. My role was being the young, impressionable college kid from Iowa who thought it was cool to hang out with one of my comedy idols. As I bragged about my adventures to friends back home, folks thought I was making this stuff up.

So I became determined to snap a picture with Farley.

My opportunity came that December at Second City's annual Christmas party for employees and alumni. Closed to the public, this was a night of celebration and revelry . . . and Chris Farley was there! I found him in the back swapping cocaine with some of the kitchen staff. He looked like he had been partying for a few days straight at that point. I jumped in with friends for a group shot, and there in the back of our photo, posing alongside us college kids, was a drunk Chris Farley.

This was the late 1990s, a bygone era before Instagram and Facebook. We didn't have digital cameras with instantly-uploadable photos. Nope. I had to head across the street to a 24-hour Walgreens to drop off my film for three-day development (three days—oh the horror!). I was excited because on that cold, wintry Monday night in Chicago's Old Town district, I had partied with Chris Farley.

Thursday morning I was sitting down for a college class when a buddy came in the door. "Hey, Herron! Did you hear about Chris Farley?" he announced. "You bet," I replied. "I just partied with him two nights ago, and I'll pick up the pictures after class!"

"No," my friend pressed on, his voice lowering a bit. "I mean, did you hear the news about Farley? They just discovered his body in the John Hancock Building."

Turns out that two nights after my photo was taken, Farley was continuing a four-day partying binge. After smoking crack and snorting heroin with a call girl, he took her back to his apartment in the John Hancock Building on Michigan Avenue. There was an argument about money that caused her to get up in a huff. Chris tried to follow but instead collapsed on the floor, struggling to breathe. His final words were, "Don't leave me." Instead of calling 9-1-1, the escort stole his watch and wrote a note saying she'd had a lot of fun, then left.

Chris Farley died alone.

2

WHAT IF TOMMY BOY LED A CHURCH?

> *"You kids are probably saying to yourselves: 'I'm gonna go out there and grab the world by the tail and wrap it around and pull it down and put it in my pocket.' Well I'm here to tell you that you're probably going to find out, as you go out there, that you're not going to amount to jack squat!"* - Chris Farley as SNL's Matt Foley: Motivational Speaker

Life got a little weird that Christmas season. Everyone at the theater was either in tears or walking around shell-shocked. National news and paparazzi were setting up cameras along North Wells, but none of us felt like talking.

My ambitions were slowly being eclipsed by the fragility of life. My front seat view of a rich, famous, rock star comedian's dramatic implosion shook me to the core. What was the point of pursuing fame? What motivates men and women to seek approval from a sea of anonymous faces? Where does true identity come from?

Soon after, I awoke to an early morning phone call. Growing up in a pastor's house, I always knew that late night and early morning phone calls meant bad news. I think that's why I dislike talking on the phone to this day; I find phone calls too stressful.

The voice on the other end of this call brought crushing news out of the blue: two young women who had been among my close friends in high school were suddenly killed in a freak car accident. Both were popular cheerleaders with promising futures. One of the girls had even been voted Homecoming Queen. They were young, beautiful, and outgoing. Now gone suddenly.

When I traveled home to Iowa for the funerals, the entire community was crushed. The suddenness juxtaposed with the finality of death rattled so many of my friends. It didn't help that the number one song at the time, Celine Dion's "My Heart Will Go On" was constantly playing on the radio.

When you witness so much tragedy in such a small span of time, you tend to reevaluate your life and question things a bit. For me, the haunting weight of my own mortality hung heavy over me. I had grown up in the church and was a follower of Christ . . . even if my Bible had inch-thick dust sitting on it.

My confusion came from my relationships in Chicago. My friends in the theater world came from all different streams: Christian, Jewish, gay, straight, atheist, Buddhist, even Muslim. I wrestled with this question for months: If everyone eventually dies (whether they're a famous comedian or homecoming queen) and all these belief systems contradict each other, which one most lines up with reality?

I spent a season of life pursuing truth. I studied all the world's varied faith systems and beliefs, reading things like the Book of Mormon, the Qu'ran, talking to all my friends, etc. I was on a quest and wouldn't stop until I found the answer.

At some point in my new journey, I began reading my Bible. I know, newsflash, right? My mind was a like a thirsty sponge, longing to engage with a deeper reality. I didn't really have a plan and flipped aimlessly through my Bible. Some passages felt familiar, but most were foreign to me.

My search spilled over into scholarly commentaries that unpacked the riches of key Bible passages. I stumbled upon one commentary written about 1 Corinthians 15. Turns out that historians point to that passage of Scripture as the first written, historical account of the life and death of Jesus Christ. Years before the four Gospels of Matthew, Mark, Luke, and John were penned, Paul of Tarsus wrote these words to the church in Corinth:

> *"For I delivered to you as of first importance what I also received: that Christ died for our sins in accordance with the Scriptures, that he was buried, that he was raised on the third day in accordance with the Scriptures . . ."* - *1 Corinthians 15:3-4 (ESV)*

Now I had grown up in the Church, sung hymns while facing a gigantic hanging cross, and even seen a couple episodes of Veggie Tales; but for some reason, these words jumped off the page at me: Jesus died and then rose by His own power from the dead! In my experience, dead people tend to stay in their casket. I've never been to a funeral that resulted in the person getting up again.

I kept reading and was struck by these words from Paul:

> *"And if Christ has not been raised, then our preaching is in vain and your faith is in vain."* - *1 Corinthians 15:14 (ESV)*

I liked this. Not because of the message but Paul's honest attitude. He wasn't here to argue or thump his chest arrogantly like I'd seen a lot of Christians on TV do. Paul was just being honest: if Jesus is still dead in the grave, then this whole Christianity thing is a joke and we should all pack up and go home.

Which is what makes verse 20 explosive:

> *"But in fact Christ has been raised from the dead, the first fruits of those who have fallen asleep!"* - 1 Corinthians 15:20 (ESV)

Bingo! That's what finally clicked for me. Scholars point to the resurrection of Jesus Christ as the singular historic event that either makes Christianity true or false. I soon discovered the archaeological, sociological, and scientific evidences for the resurrection of Christ are absolutely overwhelming.

Listen, I don't know about you, but if a guy walks around for three years saying He is God, gets tortured to death by highly-skilled executioners, and three days later rises back up by His own power, I tend to believe He is God! That's the guy I want to get behind. Give me that team jersey!

Yes, I had received Christ at an early age, but in college God became very real to me. And if God had provided the solution to identity and heartache and death, I wanted to be part of amplifying His Message.

The megaphone prepared for me was comedy. I've come to realize that all the years spent learning and performing comedy was my leadership training. Performing live comedy, like ministry, is all about relationships and trust, while creating fresh material for the stage in-the-moment entails retraining your brain to think differently.

What I've come to realize is that improvisational comedy—the kind of made-up stuff you see on shows like *Whose Line Is It Anyway?*—can help you approach leadership within the local church differently. The methods employed by comedians over the past 50 years can be leveraged to improve, or rather *improv* your leadership.

This book is an invitation to a journey. Let's approach leadership with fresh eyes.

Holy Shift is about seeing your church through a new prism and embracing challenges the way John Belushi did: like a bull in a china shop. This book won't automatically make you the funniest person in the room, but if you wrestle through *Holy Shift* honestly and sincerely, it will change how you approach life and ministry as a leader.

3

HUMOR OVER HAMMER

Kill the judge in your head and just take action. - Mick Napier

Sweat was dripping on the brows of the men as they fervently cried out to Baal. The blazing hot sun offered no shield from its mighty rays, a sensation that the people of Israel had miserably grown accustomed to during the past three years of drought.

Heeding the decree of their king, all of Israel was now assembled at the northern mountain of Carmel, overlooking the Valley of Armageddon. If you squinted, you might see the tiny town of Nazareth in the distance.

A showdown had been occurring for many hours on this historic day between the followers of Baal and one lonely prophet of God named Elijah. All of Israel was assembled on the mountain, fanning themselves and trying to remain focused on the hoarse shouts of the Baalites.

Soon they would witness something so out of the ordinary and supernatural that thousands of years later, people would still be talking about it: Elijah would pray and a wall of fire would fall down from the sky. That type of supernatural phenomenon doesn't happen everyday! If that happened in today's world, CNN would cover it live and the trending hashtag on Twitter would be #HolyFireHolyCrap!

Here's the thing: the miracle of 1 Kings 18 is not that fire fell down from heaven. I can say this with confidence because I have been to Mount Carmel in Israel and have carefully studied the ancient life of Elijah. We talk about the fire today, yet we miss what was really happening in that historical context.

Our first clue that something else is happening occurs in the opening verse of 1 Kings 18 when God says to Elijah, "Go, show yourself to Ahab, and I will send rain upon the earth." The Lord promises rain to a thirsty people. And when God makes you a promise, you can take it to the bank.

On Mount Carmel, Elijah declares, "Fill four jars with water and pour it on the burnt offering and on the wood." When they obey he says, "Do it a second time." And they do it a second time. And Elijah says, "Do it a third time." And they do it a third time. And the water ends up running around the altar and filling the trench with water.

Every time I've heard this story in church, the focus has been on the drenched altar. The wood was wet and no matchstick was going to light it. But having been to Mount Carmel, I now have a different question: Where did the jars of water come from in the first place?

When you visit Mount Carmel, you can plainly see there is no body of water in the vicinity. The geography has not radically changed in the thousands of years since the time of Elijah; the mountain has not moved. So where did all that water that drenches the altar originate?

The clue is in the king's decree: when he declares that all of Israel is to assemble at Mount Carmel to witness the showdown, the king was requiring his people to travel many, many miles on foot in the desert. There were no 7-Elevens in ancient Israel, so I'm sure you can do the math: the Israelites brought the jars of water on the journey with them to Mount Carmel.

Water meant hydration and relief. If you have water, you have life, particularly during the third year of an unyielding drought. And so Elijah's request was striking: "Fill four jars with water and pour it on the burnt offering and on the wood." Elijah got the water from the people. That was a sacrifice. The people had to be willing to give up what was most prized and valuable in that moment.

Elijah called for commitment once and some gave. He asked a second time (I imagine with a voice like Morgan Freeman): "Some of you are holding onto your water." More came forward and emptied their jars onto God's altar. Yet the Lord wanted more skin in the game for this miracle; He knew there were still some holdouts clutching their last drops of precious water.

Elijah called for commitment a third time: "You want to see God do a miracle in our generation? Pour your water on this rock." And they did it a third time. Why three (literal) altar calls? Because God always calls His people to radical sacrifice so that when the miracle occurs, only He can receive the glory.

The story continues: Elijah calls down fire from heaven with such intensity and heat that even the ground is consumed. Watching from the sidelines, the four hundred and fifty prophets of Baal collectively wet themselves (ironically providing additional hydration on the mountaintop) and Israel refocuses their attention on the one true God.

But that's not the miracle of the story.

In his moment of supreme triumph, Elijah falls to his knees and prays. His servant searches in the distance for a rain cloud, but nothing is on the horizon. Seven times Elijah fervently prays, seven times the servant scans the skies. Finally the cloud is spotted and

God's promise comes through: the heavens open with rain and the drought is over.

Here's my point: If it hasn't rained in three years, what is the last thing you want to see falling from the sky?

Fire.

The miracle is not that fire fell from the sky. The miracle is the promised rain.

Church leaders, don't miss this: it is easier to bring fire than to bring rain. We love to bring the heat and singe people with our truth-bombs. But what our people really need is rain. The people in your community and region are dehydrated. Bring refreshing rain.

Leaders set the tone and leaders go first. Elijah is the leader and he didn't see it rain after one prayer meeting. With everyone watching him intently, Elijah had to work *seven times harder* to bring the rain. And the rain was what the people of God needed most.

And what about all those people who gave their jars of water earlier; do you think they got their water back? You bet! When we sacrifice our comforts at the altar of God, the result is a blessing beyond our wildest dreams.

And the point of this story is simple: when people leave church on Sundays, they need to feel like it rained on them, not that they got burned by fire.

That is why this chapter is called, Humor Over Hammer. Any fool can bring the hammer down in the pulpit, yet that is not the tool that will best reach a thirsty generation. If you want to truly reach and engage the Millennial Generation, you might need less John MacArthur and more Jon Stewart. *Humor Over Hammer!*

DON'T FREAK OUT

"Comedy is simply a funny way of being serious." - Peter Ustinov

Some readers may have raised eyebrows and balk at the premise of this book: leveraging comedy principles for leading a church. Before some of you email your 95 Theses and blog from your mama's basement in between reruns of *The Big Bang Theory*, hear me out.

Saturday Night Live, *The Daily Show*, *The Late Show*—we've all seen the funny stuff. Oh, how we love the funny stuff. But did you know there are actually principles at work in the creation of the funny?

Every church could use a *Holy Shift*. The same principles that empower and guide comedians' minds to make our sides hurt in gushing laughter can also enhance and deepen our ability to lead people in their journeys with Christ.

Now listen, I believe in the local church. The Bible clearly teaches it is God's vessel for making Jesus famous:

> "... Through the church the manifold wisdom of God might now be made known to the rulers and authorities in the heavenly places." - Ephesians 3:10 (ESV)

I also enjoy comedy, especially its disarming power to connect universally. I've preached to hundreds of diverse audiences ranging from sophisticated teenagers in Arizona to young adults in Ohio to third-world Africans in Zambia. Same Bible, same comedy, same impact.

When comedy is leveraged in leadership and speaking, arms become uncrossed, faces smile, and hearts soften. In leadership and life, you will amplify your results when you aim for less cathedral and more comedy club.

Don't freak out: nobody is suggesting chucking the Scriptures and wearing a clown hat. The Message is unchanging, but the methods have to always be flexible and adapting.

This book is about making a *Holy Shift* and truly becoming a missionary to your region; removing all the barriers between someone far from God and the gospel. I'm not interested in the "missional" label, which is nothing more than a sub-cultural church-world fad in hipster overalls (by the way, if you have to go around telling people you're "missional," you're probably not!). Instead, I'm more interested in leveraging what enduringly touches all cultures (comedy) to produce a *Holy Shift* in the ministry approach of today's churches.

Making a *Holy Shift* requires us to think like a missionary. Missionaries stand in the gap and use the culture's language to engage people far from God. I'm here to tell you that in the 21st Century, the American culture's language is laughter. There's a reason why millennials point to Comedy Central as their main source for news and current events. There is power in speaking truth through the lens of comedy.

Let me play all my cards here: I'm a Bible guy. I hang my hat on the essentials of Christian doctrine: Jesus is God, the Bible is true, Hell is hot, and forever is a long time. Being both a seminary graduate and a former member of the Acts 29 Network, you're not going to see any rational Christian accuse me of rejecting *sola scriptura*. I believe and affirm that Scripture alone is our court of highest authority. Like I said, I'm a Bible guy.

That said, I do not believe in *solo scriptura*, the idea held by some churches that truth is exclusively and only found in Scripture and nowhere else. If this is the case, then my Bachelor of Arts degree is a wash, and my wife's Bachelor of Science degree is useless (I just like saying my wife has BS!). Neither of us studied Bible in any of our undergraduate courses, yet we possess truth from our college years.

Saint Augustine said it well hundreds of years ago:

> "A person who is a good and true Christian should realize that truth belongs to his Lord, wherever it is found, gathering and acknowledging it even in pagan literature..."[3]

All truth is God's truth. When God wants to grab the attention of leaders, He pulls out all the stops. Numbers 22:28 says, "Then the LORD gave *the donkey* the ability to speak." God used a jackass to bang home a point to one of His prophets! I don't know about you, but that's funny!

If God can speak through a donkey, it proves that He has a sense of humor and that the orthodox faith can be amplified in unorthodox ways. Comedy and church leadership can link arms.

Over the past 15+ years, I've made the *Holy Shift* as a youth pastor, a church planter, and now as the lead pastor of one of the fastest-growing churches in Michigan.

So let's all put the fun back in fundamentalism and make a *Holy Shift* together. The same recipe practiced for a half century by improvisational comedians translates well with the dynamics of leading the local church.

It's going to be fun, frustrating, and scary. But you can do it. I believe in you.

SECTION TWO
GRAB THE MIC

START WITH A YES

"The thing that always fascinated me about improv is that it's basically a happy accident that you think you're initiating. You enter a scene and decide that your character is in a bar, but your partner thinks you're performing dental surgery. The combination of those two disparate ideas melds into something that could never have been created on its own." - Tina Fey[4]

Some of the most fun I've ever had in ministry was the time we launched a brand new student ministry from scratch, and we had no idea what we were doing.

The previous senior pastor had a small vision but a penchant for racking up a ton of debt for the church. What bugged me most was that he had allowed the youth group to limp along. Mediocrity was celebrated. As the new senior pastor, it drove me crazy with a holy discontent. Psalm 71:18 tells us to declare God's glory and power to the next generation. I was not okay being the senior pastor of a church that was only reaching a small handful of teenagers.

So I hit control-alt-delete and nuked everything. I took over as youth pastor, released most of the adult volunteers, changed the gathering time and location, brought in our new worship pastor, had him work up a cover of Beyonce's "Single Ladies," and wrote a message on becoming young men and women of honor.

I circled up our adult volunteers for a single training session ahead of time and was gut-honest: "This whole experiment is going to be a mess. We have absolutely no idea what to expect, but if we stick together, I guarantee it will be fun. Just be open to trying new ideas and say 'Yes' more than you say 'No'."

We hoped and prayed that 50 teens would show up that first night.

God heard our prayer, laughed, and sent 150 teenagers. In a town of 3,000. In the middle of a Michigan cornfield.

To this day, I can say that we didn't know what we were doing. We just made it up along the way. We improvised. Our small groups were thrown together like we were building the plane as it flew through the air.

It didn't matter that it felt like mass chaos—the initial Yes became a wellspring of adrenaline and forward movement. When we chose to take a risk for the kingdom and jump off a cliff, God took what was natural for us and made it super . . . that's the essence of the supernatural! When God puts His super on our natural, life-change becomes the byproduct.

THE FUN IS FOUND
ON THE OTHER SIDE OF YES

"Leaders are visionaries with a poorly developed sense of fear and no concept of the odds against them." - Robert Jarvik

Your first step toward a *Holy Shift* is to think like a comedian and grab the microphone. The most basic rule and premise of creating comedy is agreement. Radical agreement.

When you're improvising on the fly, this means you are required to agree with whatever your partner has created and thrown out there. Always agree with a Yes.

When two performers agree in the moment, the scene moves forward. To create a *Holy Shift*, your default must be to start with a Yes.

When you start with a Yes, you will generate ideas faster and more efficiently. Yes-thinking helps you pivot out of tight and uncomfortable spaces at church by creating agreement and a shared path forward.

"No" grinds invention, innovation, and forward-movement to a screeching halt. Pressing into the Yes reminds you to respect what your partner has created and to start from an open-minded place. The fun is found on the other side of Yes.

I am the founding pastor of Life Church Michigan which serves the Great Lakes Bay Region of the High Five State. Launched on St. Patrick's Day in 2013, we are one church in two locations growing faster than water on mogwai.

I get asked all the time why our church is growing so fast when we started with absolutely no people and no money. The answer is simple: I believe deep down in my core that Christ followers are given the mission by God to reach the lost at any cost. Because of that passion, I am willing to do whatever it takes to reach people who normally will not darken a church door.

As goes the leader, so goes the church. If you want your people to be fired up about reaching out and making heaven crowded, look in the mirror, because it starts with you!

I am convinced that non-distracting excellence is absolutely key to impacting irreligious people. If you want to reach exhausted people with God's inexhaustible grace, you need to think about first impressions.

When someone visits Life Church for the first time, we have about seven minutes to make a lasting impact on them before they've sized us up and made up their mind about any future visits. Until someone is environmentally-secure, they will not become theologically-aware.

If our church environment doesn't reach a threshold of attainable credibility in the eyes of a person far from God, they will put their invisible force fields up and completely miss the message of hope and grace.

Music is a big hurdle for church visitors. In our age of iTunes, music is the language of this generation. So during the first year of Life Church, I knew that recruiting a world-class worship leader was going to be mission-critical.

The only problem was that we were a start-from-scratch church plant with a handful of people, a rented elementary school to use on Sunday mornings, and no money. We had no denomination or mega-church funding us with loads of cash or releasing to us a bunch of people. All we had was a vision, calcium in the spine, and the philosophy to "Go until you get a 'No'!"

I posted a nationwide ad for the worship position, whispered a prayer, and began to weed through the videos and resumes that began pouring in. Nothing connected and I started to feel hopeless.

In the meantime, we contracted touring worship bands to play for us which we discovered could be a very hit-and-miss process. Because we were essentially renting outside bands' services, you never could predict what kind of quality (or lack thereof) to expect during worship on Sunday mornings. It was like a game of Worship Whack-A-Mole complete with skinny jeans and scarves.

I continued plowing through resumes but could not find the right fit for our next worship leader and we were running out of patience with Rent-A-Bands. The butterflies in my stomach were growing to the size of Mothra, my attitude was shifting from hope to fear, and I was sweating more than Mike Tyson in a Spelling Bee.

That's when I felt the Holy Spirit speak to me.

Have you ever heard God's voice?

In the Bible, God's voice sometimes sounds like a tornado and other times like a whisper.

I've discovered that the Holy Spirit sounds unmistakably like my wife.

One night after ~~whining~~ lamenting (lamenting sounds more biblical, right?) about my fruitless search, my wife turned to me and said, "Really? You believe that God doesn't have the right guy out there for us?"

Those were the words I needed to hear. The next day I texted an old friend from the past: "Can I call you in 10 minutes?" I picked up the phone and made a shot-in-the-dark call. And fresh air was blown into an old friendship.

We set up a Skype appointment for a few days later where I shot straight with my old buddy. To be involved with a start-from-scratch church, it involves inherent risks and increased scrutiny from naysayers in the local Christian community, but we had a big vision for the future backed up with a strong track record and solid personal integrity.

We spent the next few days praying, talking, and seeking God. Before I knew it, he said yes and his family began making plans to move across a couple states to frigid Michigan to serve at Life Church.

At the end of the day, it came down to my friend boldly making a *Holy Shift*: Start with a Yes. They didn't allow praying about it to become a cover for indecisiveness. He made a choice and moved forward.

Did it mean taking a huge leap of faith, walking away from security and a big paycheck, and cannonballing into the deep end of the pool? Absolutely.

If you're thinking that they could have used someone playing Devil's Advocate during their decision-making process, allow me to stop you right there: the Devil doesn't need an advocate! What we need are more men and women in the local church who boldly Start with a Yes.

Yes carries an element of fear, but fear is just hope looking backward. If the thought of starting with a Yes stirs up anxiety within you, understand that anxiety is just smoke. The fire is something that has become too important to you.

Starting with a Yes forces you to let go and courageously move forward. It kills paralysis and carries with it a unique combination of clarity and whimsy. In life, church, and leadership, start with a Yes and see where that takes you.

FOLLOW YOUR DREAMS

"You have the right to follow your dreams. I'm giving you permission to follow your dreams." - Martin de Maat

Years ago, back in the time when the new big thing was internet dial-up that charged by the minute, I entered my very first youth ministry job in a very old church building. The building was so old that 1560 called and wanted their worship style back. Back in the early 1900's, it had seen sunnier days as the hub of city culture and life-change. Now, however, it was pretty much a quiet little church with decaying pews that shared a distinctive smell with the Chicago subway system: wet rat.

One of the very first Sunday mornings that I was on staff, my wife arrived in the sanctuary early. As she sat quietly in the empty, echoing cathedral, she heard the sound of people approaching. The combination of Charlie Brown "Wah-Wah" talking and heels clickety-clacking down the aisle alerted her that a trio of little old church ladies were making their way toward her pew.

Suddenly the clickety-clacks stopped. There was a pregnant pause of awkward silence. Then the tenor of the chatter dropped two octaves down to a low bass. A voice rose up behind her: "She is sitting in our pew—what nerve!" Um, ya. Within six months we left that church job.

When I read stories in the Bible, I encounter a Jesus who attracted crowds and spoke life over people with compassion and hope:

> "The thief comes only to steal and kill and destroy. I came that they may have life and have it abundantly." - John 10:10 (ESV)

Abundant, amplified life! The mark of churches should be that guests walk away from a worship experience overflowing and bubbling with life, not judgment and negativity.

Over the years, I've had the honor of meeting countless other little old church ladies who cracked me up with their faith, spunk, and zest . . . all overflowing from a life impacted by Jesus. Tradition was part of their journey, but it wasn't their destination. These seasoned citizens added fuel to my fire and were always open to dreaming up new possibilities.

You see, there is a vast difference between tradition and traditionalism. Tradition is the living faith passed on from the dead. Traditionalism is the dead faith passed on from the living. In our earlier church, traditionalism had swallowed up those little old church ladies' sense of fun. Traditionalism stamps out Yes and replaces it with a hideous form of No: "But we've always done it this way."

How many church business meetings have you been part of that stamped out dreams and ideas for advancing the Kingdom:

> "But we don't have the money."

> "But we've never done that before."

> "But that might anger a family in our congregation."

Listen, nobody wants to see your "but!" Your "but" is big, ugly, and stinks. Nobody likes big buts (except Sir Mix-a-lot, but that's another story). Your big but kills passion. Your but is like a thief that seeks to steal and kill and destroy. Stop butting into progress and start with a Yes!

Whatever the problem, be part of the solution! Creative collaboration is all about giving gifts. Live comedians always seek ways to support the scene and one's fellow players with gifts. In comedy, giving gifts is the most productive move there is. Those who do it most consistently become our leaders. Affirming plus giving gifts leads to forward progress.

"So if we're improvising and I say, 'Freeze, I have a gun,' and you say, 'That's not a gun. It's your finger. You're pointing your finger at me,' our improvised scene has ground to a halt.

"But if I say, 'Freeze, I have a gun!' and you say, 'The gun I gave you for Christmas! How dare you!' then we have started a scene because we have AGREED that my finger is in fact a Christmas gun.

As an improviser, I always find it jarring when I meet someone in real life whose first answer is no: 'No, we can't do that.' 'No, that's not in the budget.' 'No, I will not hold your hand for a dollar.' What kind of way is that to live?" - Tina Fey[5]

DREAMERS AND VISIONARIES

"When you have come to the edge of all light that you know and are about to drop off into the darkness of the unknown, Faith is knowing one of two things will happen: there will be something solid to stand on or you will be taught to fly."- Patrick Overton

The very first sermon preached about Jesus is found in Acts 2 when the gifts of the Spirit were unleashed. Crowds gathered and pointed at the apostles, joking about how they must be drunk. Peter rose up, rolled up his sleeves and began his very first sermon with these words: "We're not drunk!" I've never been to a church that opened with those words.

Peter goes on to quote an obscure prophet from the Hebrew Testament named Joel.

> "And in the last days it shall be, God declares, that I will pour out my Spirit on all flesh, and your sons and your daughters shall prophesy, and your young men shall see visions, and your old men shall dream dreams." Acts 2:17 (ESV)

I love this! The very first sermon ever preached about Jesus says that the Church is supposed to be a movement of dreamers and visionaries! And don't miss this: it's not just the young people who are empowered by God to cast vision, but also the little old church ladies who "shall dream dreams."

Our mandate is to reach the lost at any cost. The Father has given us the best tool in the tool belt, His Spirit. As we reach out with the intentions of making heaven crowded, we are given permission to try new methods and embrace changing ministry techniques.

We are to approach God's Message as unchanging while handling it with the skills of MacGyver: always grabbing duct tape, pliers, and a magnifying glass to create new, innovative possibilities for amplifying the Message.

I firmly believe this first *Holy Shift* can tap into the deadest of churches and ignite a movement of leadership. When everyone on your team is willing to start with a "Yes," it places your entire church into a posture of humility, acceptance, creativity, and intentional trust. When we affirm instead of giving a knee-jerk denial, things move forward and the fun is discovered in the process.

THAT TIME SOMEONE GAVE US A FREE BUILDING

Our church is brimming with young twenty-somethings which means we have lots of couples and wedding celebrations. I don't officiate many weddings due to my busy schedule.

Recently a young lady in our church named Hannah persistently asked me to officiate her wedding. She would not give up: she would go until she got a no!

When I learned that Hannah's fiancee was in the Navy, she found my soft spot. As the son of legal immigrants, I have a deep love of country and I highly respect families in the armed services. So I said yes to officiating the wedding.

Weeks later we sat down for wedding planning and I asked, "Where do you wish to get married?"

Hannah's response puzzled me: "Oh, well our family has a church in Midland, Michigan."

I didn't understand. I thought we were their church!

"No, our family *has* a church in Midland. We literally *own* a church building!"

Fast-forward to the wedding rehearsal and I parked my car in front of an empty church building located 10 minutes from the bustling heart of Midland, Michigan. Midland was recently honored as the #1 Place to Raise a Family in Michigan. With real estate so coveted and expensive in the Midland area, how did this little gem of a church end up sitting here empty?

As we ran through the motions of the wedding rehearsal, I looked around in disbelief. I couldn't believe this building that had once housed an aging United Methodist congregation had quietly died out. You hear stories on the news all the time of churches that close their doors and leave empty shells behind . . . and I was standing in one of them.

Hannah's parents are in the real estate business and had bought the lucrative property a few years earlier because they wanted the former Manse as a rental property (back in the day, old school churches provided on-site housing for preachers). The land deal included this empty church building, and so Hannah had been right: her family owned a church building!

As the wedding rehearsal came to a close, Hannah's parents came to thank me for finding time to officiate their daughter's wedding and to let me know that I could expect an honorarium check after the wedding.

In that moment, I felt God whisper in my ear, "Go for it!" With boldness, I responded:

"How about instead of giving me a check, let me have this church building for free to launch a second campus of Life Church?"

They said Yes!

Because I said Yes to officiating a wedding, I walked into a divine opportunity.

Because I said Yes to God's whisper, I walked out with a signed contract for a free church building!

There is power when you Start with a Yes. Don't talk yourself out of a move of God! Start with a Yes and watch the miracle unfold!

YES, AND

"I am giving you permission to succeed." - Martin de Maat

The top-grossing comedy of 1984 was a motion picture about a business start-up. The line of work was catching ghosts. The chemistry of the cast combined with a punchy script led to a movie still cheered today.

Here's the interesting thing: the *Ghostbusters* movie we know today wasn't what was originally intended. Writers Dan Aykroyd and Harold Ramis originally wrote *Ghostbusters* as a time-traveling feature with a greater emphasis on horror and sci-fi. The stars of the film were originally going to be John Belushi and John Candy.

As pre-production casting progressed, the script changed. Comedic scenes were rewritten and improved upon. The story was deepened and expanded based on input from their production team. What was already funny became funnier. New directions led to some key casting changes. Bill Murray and Rick Moranis were invited to join the cast. Their chemistry added vast richness to the classic movie we enjoy today.

What is the moral of this story? After you start with a Yes, heighten the initiation with Yes, And.

Can you imagine a world without Bill Murray's sly Peter Venkman or Rick Moranis' uber-nerd, Louis Tulley? If Aykroyd and Ramis had remained rigidly hardened to their original script treatment, *Ghostbusters* would have become a tangled mess of a time-traveling freak show.

Instead, they were flexible enough to embrace new ideas for the script and casting which heightened the premise with a fun new direction (Yes, And) that reached a broader audience.

The first attempt at writing a script wasn't the final answer. The paradigm shift to the *Ghostbusters* we know today contains the recipe for a classic. The question is whether or not your church leadership is flexible along the journey.

MAKE IT BETTER

"Say 'Yes' as often as you can. When I was starting out in Chicago, doing improvisational theater with Second City, I was taught to 'Yes, And,' which means that you go onstage to improvise a scene with no script, you have no idea what's going to happen, maybe with someone you've never met before. To build a scene, you have to accept what the other improviser initiates on stage. They say you're doctors . . . you're doctors! And then you add to that: we're doctors AND we're trapped in an ice cave. That's Yes, And. By following each other's lead, neither of you are really in control. It's more of a mutual discovery than a solo adventure. What happens in a scene is often as much a surprise to you as it is to the audience." - Stephen Colbert

Yes, And takes the original initiation (Start with a Yes) and heightens it (Yes, And). Adding an And helps your team make it better!

Like adding gasoline to fire, Yes, And has the explosive power to generate tremendous energy. You agree and then add something of your own. Have a take. Be someone. Stand for something. Rock your style. What your style is doesn't matter nearly as much as whether or not you rock it.

Yes, And is the rocket fuel of comedy writing and leading a team. If your partner starts with, "I can't believe it's so hot in here," and you answer with a simple one-word "Yup," the scene has stalled out. You've given your partner nothing to work with, which puts him back in his head instead of being in the moment. If instead you Yes, Anded with, "What did you expect? We're in hell!" things keep moving forward.

The first improvisers and comedy writers back in the 1950's learned that saying No to ideas stops creativity and leadership. No pushes people away. As a leader, you want to walk toward people, not away.

This is why Yes, And is so powerful! Yes, And accepts ideas as a gift: "I've got your back, thank you for the idea-gift; let's move forward together in faith." Today's world looks down on Yes-Men, yet Yes-Men are who make us laugh!

Trust is built through Yes, which is essential as you are journeying out into the unknown together. Trust eclipses fear. Many times, improvisers (and church leaders) fear the consequences of their own actions and as a result, freeze, or stick to safe-but-boring actions and scenes. I'm urging you to cannonball into the deep end of the pool and just do something, anything, and see where it leads while improvising.

Yes, And takes things to the next level. When someone suggests an idea or new direction, Yes, And not only empowers but creates partnership.

I witnessed the power of Yes, And in 1997 when Second City's Kevin Dorff and Scott Adsit improvised a scene about driver's ed.

> KEVIN: *"In the state of Illinois, in order to obtain a driver's license, we need to test you in your 'real world' driving ability. Let's begin that phase of the test by having you put the car in drive. And proceed. Now, uh, please remove your seat belt."*

(Scott hesitates, with a puzzled look, then obliges.)

KEVIN: "When should you wear your seat belt?"

SCOTT: "Whenever I get in the car."

KEVIN: "No, whenever you get pulled over."

Scott never pushed back on Kevin's words, he just went with it and took each idea to its logical yet outrageous conclusion (Yes, And). When Kevin instructed his student to practice eating fast food while behind the wheel, Scott demonstrated Yes, And by chowing down a cheeseburger and fries with his hands while simultaneously steering with his knee!

The comedy came naturally as Kevin heightened each hurdle for his driver's education student to accomplish:

KEVIN: "Now let me see you apply this make-up while you drive."

SCOTT: "I don't really wear make-up."

KEVIN: "I'm sorry, but there is no gender bias allowed on this test!"

Kevin drove the scene forward with suggestions that Scott would Yes, And memorably. In the comedy world, Yes, And is a rule that heightens someone's idea and super-sizes the gift they present you with. This same rule works in leadership. When an idea is thrown out to you, Yes, And produces movement and possibility.

YES, AND MADE LIFE CHURCH GO VIRAL

I'm always skeptical when I hear a church leader say that something they said or did "went viral." To me, trending online and going viral is a very high bar to jump over. And yet heading toward Christmas of 2015, our Yes, And made a church outreach idea literally go viral.

Let me back-up by taking you to the Election of 2012. In the dust and chaos of last-minute presidential campaigning, a brief press release from The Walt Disney Company all but disappeared amidst the busy news cycle.

George Lucas, creator of *Star Wars*, had sold *Lucasfilm* to the House of Mouse.

Immediately a light bulb went off in my head: there's going to be new *Star Wars* films! The internet is going to go nuts!

Then a second, crazier idea popped into my imagination: what if we leveraged what would become the highly-anticipated movie premiere buzz of Episode 7 for Kingdom purposes? What if we rented out a whole movie theater for the premiere of the new *Star Wars* film?

Fast-forward to 2015 and I pitched the idea to our team. Everyone thought it was just crazy enough to reach some more people far from God. We started with a Yes.

And then the team started to Yes, And: they heightened the initial idea of giving away movie tickets and layered it with plans for a whole Christmas message series that incorporated elements of the Star Wars story and connected it to the true story of Christ's birth.

Heading toward the busy Christmas season, we announced the coming of literal Stormtroopers dancing in Life Kids, make-your-own lightsaber kits for visiting families, and our free giveaway of movie tickets to the premiere.

That's when the local newspaper called. They asked if they could do a brief story on our church's unique approach to ministry. Starting with a Yes, I did the interview, posed for the photographer, and thought nothing of it.

On the morning of December 3, 2015, the headline was posted on the local news site: *Michigan church using 'Star Wars Christmas' to attract millennials.* By that afternoon, there were television news crews in our church parking lot.

Turns out that the article was picked up by The Associated Press and literally went viral. Our two-year-old church start-up was suddenly being talked about on the websites of Time Magazine, USA Today, The Washington Times, The Houston Chronicle . . . everywhere!

Talk radio hosts in California and Virginia were buzzing about this fun outreach idea, The Detroit News sent reporters to our worship experiences, and Washington DC's AP Bureau called asking for an interview.

All this attention translated into record-breaking crowds every Sunday leading up to Christmas and nearly 100 people placing their trust in Jesus Christ!

You don't have to take my word for it: Google the four words "Star Wars Michigan Church" and see for yourself!

UNANIMITY IS OVERRATED

> "The audience laughs at agreement . . . a secret of comedy that very few people realize." - Del Close

You may be thinking, "But Jon (there's that ugly 'but' again!), you haven't met my board! They would never dream of Yes, Anding changes in our church. It would require a unanimous vote!"

In early 1999, I attended a special pre-screening of the then soon-to-be-released motion picture, *Analyze This*, starring Billy Crystal and Robert DeNiro. The late Harold Ramis (Egon of *Ghostbusters* fame) was on-hand afterward as the film's director for a Q&A with the crowd.

I lined up behind everyone else to ask Mr. Ramis my one film question into the booming microphone. Everyone else asked things like, "What was it like working with Billy Crystal and Robert DeNiro?" I had a different intention. I stepped up to the microphone and asked my deep, life-changing question for the celebrated writer and director: "When are we going to see a *Ghostbusters 3*?" To my surprise, my question was met with raucous applause.

When the cheering subsided, Harold Ramis responded kindly, "We have a script and we're waiting on Bill (Murray) to read it. We want unanimity."

That was 1999. Nearly 20 years later and we have seen no Ghostbusters 3. Ramis, Aykroyd, and the gang waited and waited for Murray to read the script to ensure unanimity until sadly in early 2014, Harold Ramis passed away and the dreams of a third Ghostbusters installment gave way to a complete reboot of the movie in 2016.

Fifteen years of waiting for unanimity led to a missed opportunity.

Desiring 100 percent unanimous group agreement can stall or kill momentum. It paralyzes progress by requiring every single person to personally sign-off while sometimes resulting in the addition of personal agendas. That produces sausage; nobody enjoys watching sausage being made.

Here's a shocker: nowhere in the Bible do we see an example of a *Robert's Rules of Order* resulting in a vote that leads to unanimity. None of that is in the Bible—mandating unanimity in church leadership is just man-made traditionalism that popped up hundreds of years later. That's not to say that dear old Robert is a bad guy, just that the traditionalism almost always prevents forward motion. Voting and unanimity are code for Bill Murray stalling tactics.

The other problem with waiting for unanimity is someone always loses. Either the idea loses because there's a hold out or somebody on your team gets bruised when they discover they're in the minority.

Remember the story I shared about that time someone gave us a free building? I didn't put the idea for a new campus up for a vote because I didn't want there to be winners and losers. In fact, with a clear vision for future campuses and a free building being offered, I didn't need to create buy-in. I just championed it and the consensus followed!

Group consensus and agreement is modeled in the Bible and creates forward motion and energy. Consensus promotes faith and trust in one another, creating a shared, beautiful experience. Consensus, setting aside personal agendas, produces sizzling bacon. And everybody enjoys the taste and smells of bacon.

Yes, And opens the doorway toward exciting new places as a leader. T.E. Lawrence (a.k.a. Lawrence of Arabia) once wrote:

"All men dream, but not equally. Those who dream by night in the dusty recesses of their minds awake to the day to find it was all vanity. But the dreamers of the day are dangerous men, for they may act out their dreams with open eyes, to make it possible."

SIMPLY YES, AND

Mark Sutton and Joe Bill perform the very popular *Bassprov* in Chicago. It's just two guys sitting in a boat, drinking beer, and having a conversation.

They play the same characters every time they perform. The audience immediately understands the scenario: two friends having a conversation during an absent-minded activity. Genius. Any lull in the conversation and they can ask for a beer or talk about their bait.

They're not reinventing the wheel. They're letting you eavesdrop. And that's often the most entertaining theater.

Yes, And isn't complex. You don't have to sit in a dark, smoky room and hammer out crazy ideas until the wee hours of the morning. Comedy and leadership are more about simplicity. Reducing complexity creates opportunities. Just look at the wild success of Apple, Google, and Ikea: clean and simple.

The Second City theater doesn't have a huge, commanding stage with dozens of props and elaborate staging. Overhead has been reduced with very little paint on the walls and a bare stage.

The secret to fifty years of celebrated comedy has been three chairs and a team of actors in agreement. It is amazing the adventures you can have with your team when everyone is committed to Yes, And.

Creative leadership doesn't have to be sophisticated with a big budget when a simple one will do. Improvisation is not anti-sophistication; it just teaches that simplicity is the ultimate sophistication.

The secret is not more tools at your disposal. Yes, And is the most basic of tools for teams to move the ball forward. As you move forward with whimsical agreements, fun discoveries mark the journey and will bond your team together.

Try it at your next meeting. Simply initiate with Yes, And. Agree and heighten all your conversations. The waters won't part until the heel of your foot hits the surface.

If someone initiates with a bold idea or fresh approach, what's your reaction?

>Yes, And creates possibility; No unplugs dreams.

>Yes, And empowers; No judges.

>Yes, And accepts input as gifts; No rejects future ideas.

>Yes, And builds bridges; No puts you at the bottom of any A-1 party list.

Yes, And is what moves both improv-comedy scenes and prevailing churches forward. No stops everything dead in the tracks with paralyzing fear.

When you're creating something out of nothing, Yes, And is cement for the fresh new bricks. Yes, And propels the future into motion.

No or Yes, But are popular in church committees and meetings because they allow one party to maintain control of an idea or conversation. Control is an illusion; if control guaranteed success, every church in America would be wildly successful!

Anybody can douse a passionate fire with, "No, we can't." Can you come alongside the initiator and instead say, "Yes, And?" See where it might take you.

5

THINK ENSEMBLE

"You know what intimacy is? It's into-me-you-see." - Martin de Maat

The original pioneers of improv-comedy in the 1950s included now-famous names like Alan Arkin, Mike Nichols, and a very young Joan Rivers. A famous story from the annals of Second City recounts how Rivers was once onstage and asked for an audience suggestion for a scene.

When "marriage" was shouted back, Joan initiated the scene by saying, "I want a divorce." Joan's on-stage partner said Yes, And to her initiation by saying, "What about the children?" Joan shot back, "We don't have any children!"

Of course, there was a big laugh from the audience, but Rivers' cheap laugh set up her partner—and the scene—for failure. Her denial of his reality killed the scene and ended the team's collaboration. She destroyed more than future possibilities in the scene; Rivers denied and destroyed the trust between partners.

Moving beyond Starting with Yes, I want you to Think Ensemble. Team work makes the dream work.

In the comedy world, you are taught to always, always, always make your partner look good. It's not about sharing the spotlight; it's about moving the spotlight completely off of yourself and more brightly onto everyone else on the stage. It's the comedic equivalent of valuing community.

Improvisation is about serving your partner instead of being out there and showing off. Have you ever watched an episode of *Whose Line Is It Anyway?* Have you noticed how the comics don't have time to sit down, write out their ideas, memorize lines, re-write lines? It's because they Start with a Yes and build on the idea by thinking ensemble.

You don't know what is going to come out of your partner's mouth—whatever they say in an improv scene instantly becomes the reality of the scene. Therefore, you want to build a net of trust to leap into—and that trust is knit together by the knowledge that you will always support one another, no matter what.

When you think ensemble, your church will build effective teams, break down silos, and foster creativity. Ensemble gives you an instantaneous advantage with different situations; the outcome isn't dependent on one lone person. Thinking ensemble strengthens the Body.

Think of an ensemble as a baseball team. You don't want to load your roster with all sluggers. You need different points of view and complementary strengths. Diversity is the key to thinking ensemble.

The enemies of thinking ensemble are the need to be right, stealing focus, and appearing to be in control. Jesus' disciples were always short-circuiting things when they felt the need to be right (Peter), tried stealing the focus (James and John), or were appearing to be in control (Judas the treasurer).

Ensemble is hard, but rewarding. When nobody cares who gets the credit, your team is able to explore and heighten new ideas together. When you think of winning sports teams, the championship is won not by a single athlete, but by a team of players working together. The burden is shared and the win is shared. When you think ensemble, you are freed to walk into a meeting and bring a brick, not a cathedral.

RECOGNIZE YOU'RE NOT ALONE

My friend Martin de Maat grew up at Second City. His aunt was one of improv's pioneering teachers in the 1960s, so Martin was always hanging around the theater, washing dishes, picking up the Rules of Comedy. By the late 1980s, Martin was named the Artistic Director of Second City, founding the Training Center and directly teaching comedy to the likes of Julia Louis-Dreyfuss, Chris Farley, and Steve Carrell.

Martin was also an associate professor at my alma mater, Columbia College. When I enrolled, I had no idea that I would be receiving a generous double-dose of improv training both at Second City and at Columbia. To say that Martin de Maat had a profound impact on my life would be an understatement. He was not only my professor and mentor, he was a close friend who stood by my side as a groomsman at our wedding.

Dr. de Maat taught me so much not only about improvisational comedy, but more importantly, about the joy of doing life together. I'll elaborate on Martin's wisdom in a later chapter, but for our purposes, I want to highlight Martin's core conviction that we must choose to do life together.

"What happens . . . in being with each other in acceptance and Yes Anding each other, is that you as an individual start to believe in yourself because you begin to see yourself in the others' eyes.

Your ensemble, your group, your team, your committee, is the one that's believing in you and you pull it together to do it for them.

You know, it's simply recognizing you're not alone. It's love and unconditional acceptance. You put yourself in a place of support, unconditional acceptance and love for who you are, the way you are and your uniqueness, and what you do is grow. You surround yourself with people who are truly interested in you and listen to you, and you will grow.

And it doesn't take much to start advancing you, it doesn't take much of that support, it doesn't take much of that love and that care and you can do it. You can play act with people. You can be in a state of play together." - Martin de Maat

This is how comedians move forward in front of a live audience without a script. Yes, And leads to trust, which leads to thinking ensemble with contagious unity, which leads to childlike creativity. It's how leaders might lead teams in the 21st Century.

If Martin were here right now advising you on your organization, I'll bet he would implore you not to settle for the loneliness of leadership isolation. Dream and strive for a team of church leaders who are accepting of one another's uniqueness. After all, we each bring different strengths to the table.

I love what Martin would say about the group dynamics of thinking ensemble:

> "There's a lot of laughter that goes on. Since we're laughing together, we're true community. It's a very safe place to confront your fears. The minute somebody says, 'Perform!' your fear comes up..."

As we Start with a Yes and Think Ensemble, leaders begin to embrace contagious unity and laughter. Can you imagine how your team's leadership capacity would increase if everyone was refusing to perform and instead choosing raw, authentic community? Our churches would move forward at a higher, deeper, more spiritually-sensitive level than before—a true *Holy Shift*.

TRUST US, THIS IS ALL MADE UP

> "As soon as a move is made, it's almost like dominoes just start falling because now these other things have to be true."
> - T.J. Jagodowski

Recently, I caught the indie film *Trust Us, This Is All Made Up* on the Documentary Channel. Following Chicago improvisers David Pasquesi and T.J. Jagodowski, the film unpacks the partnership "mind-meld" that occurs between two men creating live comedy on the fly.

Any leadership team—particularly pioneering tribes constantly creating new material (pastors!)—would benefit from not only the improvised performance in the film, but also the behind-the-scenes moments at the very beginning.

David and T.J. perform with absolute trust in one another—a hallmark of improvised comedy. You have to trust your partner when there is no script.

Trust is a constant dance between two supporting partners, inviting the mind to revert to preschool playtime as adults. That is where great comedy naturally flows from and collaboration naturally takes root.

The two continually work at getting into each other's minds, trying to understand how each other thinks so as to anticipate and develop deeper trust when on stage. For example, they take a day to observe NYC, spontaneously verbalizing whatever flows through their mind at that moment. This helps the other partner better understand his train of thought, which translates to greater trust and creative anticipation later on stage. Fascinating.

The rules of improvisational comedy apply to church planting and prevailing church leadership cultures. What's the key to synergy? Think Ensemble. Make the other people look good, not yourself. Support their reality. *Yes, And* their initiations.

RELATIONSHIPS ARE NOT DISPOSABLE IN A FACEBOOK WORLD

Thinking ensemble looks easy on paper but is hard in real life. Why? Because we live in the time of Facebook and Twitter, two mighty platforms that can amplify messages—and amplify grudges—if handled immaturely. And believe me, social media can be like crack for immaturity addicts.

I have a theory: we never really leave middle school. That short season of life where the awkwardness of adolescence collides with our first tastes of personal responsibility follows us through life.

Many men are still that boy in the junior high locker room comparing (more on that in a later chapter) and many women walk through life fearful of others' opinions. We have the popular kids (Hollywood), the geeks (ComicCon), need for cooler toys (Amazon), and petty schoolyard fights (political races). We never really leave middle school.

Social media simply amplifies our inner middle school angst. Angry at someone? Technology doesn't force you to seek reconciliation; you can simply "UnFollow" them. They won't even know. Facebook has made relationships disposable, just another product to consume and spit out.

That's why thinking ensemble is so explosive: relationships are vital toward forward progress. When you sign up to be a leader, you sign up for conflict. Thinking ensemble directs you to walk toward the people there is conflict with, not away from them (you can't support someone you're not talking to). In the Bible, we read these words about conflict:

> "For we do not wrestle against flesh and blood, but against the rulers, against the authorities, against the cosmic powers over this present darkness, against the spiritual forces of evil in the heavenly places." Ephesians 6:12 (ESV)

The Gospel reminds us that we are messy humans who easily fall into sin. Our flesh can sometimes seek to judge before our spirit listens. But Ephesians 6:12 reminds us that if it has flesh and blood, it is not your enemy.

If you are holding anger toward someone, that person is not your enemy. They are a human being created in the image of God whom Jesus already died for and the Father has already declared to be not guilty. Reconciliation is not something you can put off. Biblically, it is always for today.

As I gently remind our church periodically, the Internet is an online tool for building community, but should never be used for tearing it down. If you ever feel wronged by someone (a fellow Christ follower, a church staff member, a pastor, etc.), posting your grievance online is never the correct course of action. In fact, if someone is willing to attack another person through a blog hiding behind flickering pixels but refuses to meet with them in person, we have a word for that: coward.

For example, there was a stay-at-home dad with too much time on his hands and a chip on his shoulder who self-righteously took it upon himself to minutely critique and obsess from a distance over every movement I made as the leader of Life Church. He had never once stepped foot in our church, was not a part of our ministry, and had never even met my family, yet his angry public tweets escalated toward taking unwarranted shots at my children.

While editing this book at our local deli in town, I looked up from my MacBook and was surprised to see Mr. Grouchy-Pants waiting in line for his to-go order. Seeing an opportunity to connect in real life, I got up and grabbed a spot in line directly behind him.

Before I could offer him a simple, "Hello," he darted a fast glance in my direction and quickly looked away. I stood amazed as he morphed into the Mac spinning color wheel: silently frozen and robotic. The guy would not turn to look in my direction! He quickly took his to-go order and slid out a side door.

The moral of this story: never say something on social media that you would not say with someone standing right next to you. You never know when that might happen!

The Internet is the last place you should be when you're upset or working through an issue. When you are angry, you will always make the best speech you will ever regret. Every time there is a disagreement between people in the Bible, the antidote is to meet with the person quickly, quietly, and gracefully.

Here are some simple, biblical principles on how to gracefully confront someone with the aim of restoring the relationship.

- Never attempt to resolve a problem over the phone, via email, on Facebook, texting, or online. Meet in person! Pixels on a screen hide the nuances of body language and vocal inflections.

- Deal with any problem immediately—that day! Letting something fester invites the enemy.

- There is no room for grudges among Christ-followers. Grudges imprison you and create a distorted lens for experiencing reality.

- Gossip tears down. Transparent grace builds up.

- Be quick to listen and slow to speak.

- You can choose to either believe the best about a person's motives or assume the worst. The former builds trust over the long haul.

- Humility is contagious. Humility builds bridges.

- Asking for forgiveness is a freeing experience. Offering forgiveness is a freeing experience. Both bring you and the other person closer together in relationship.

- Bitterness does not lead toward wholeness:

    "Bitterness creates an illusion of control and power. Bitterness is a form of hate. It is anger facing backwards. When we are embittered toward someone, we hold him prisoner to an experience or action in the past. In our minds our bitterness holds him captive and does not allow him to move forward. The reality is that our bitterness traps no one but ourselves. If the offender genuinely seeks forgiveness, even when you are unwilling to give it, he or she is made free. The only person you keep trapped in yesterday when you are unwilling to forgive is yourself." – Erwin McManus[6]

BELIEVE THE BEST

Introverts make great communicators. I learned this while studying under Tina Fey who is smart, polite, and sharp as a tack. And an introvert.

Tina wasn't the after-party girl at Second City. Instead she labored through and internalized ideas during her off-hours until they came out on stage as comedic genius.

Years later this idea about introverts was drilled into my mind again by John Piper at a 2004 pastors conference. He declared that introverts make great preachers because God's grace eclipses their weakness. Piper thanks God to this day for his awkward teenage years. According to him, they were the fertile genesis of digging deep toward a pastoral soul.

Introverted leaders can be easily misunderstood because of how they are naturally wired: strong on-stage while quietly recharging off-stage. Misunderstandings are common when you're in the public eye as a comedian or leader.

Whether it's mistaking an introvert for an extrovert or observing three minutes out of someone's day and assuming it is how they behave 24/7, we all have a choice to make in how we relate to people. The key is to not assume the worst about someone but instead to always believe the best.

MY BRUSH WITH THE PILLSBURY DOUGHBOY

Sometimes when I'm listening to the radio or hearing the voice of a cartoon character, I try to imagine what the person behind the voice looks like in real life. For example, does the voice-over artist for *Alvin and the Chipmunks* look like a little kid? Is the *Geico* gecko really an Englishman? Is the radio DJ I'm listening to fresh out of college or about to retire?

It's always difficult to walk in the truth without the whole story. When we choose to believe the best, we are trusting others with an ensemble mindset.

During a college class, I remember our professor announcing that we would soon have a special guest lecturer: the voice behind the Pillsbury Doughboy! This sent our imaginations racing as we all attempted to guess what he might look like based on what little information we had.

Based on all those brief commercials I had seen and a few rumors I had heard, I assumed he would be a childlike, short, pasty fellow who invited one and all to poke his muffin belly for a pudgy laugh.

But that's the problem when we don't assume the best about people. More often than not, we're wrong.

In improvisation, you must believe the best about your partners. As a leader who is a follower of Christ, we must also strive to live in truth and grace. Sometimes I can stray when I don't believe the best about people. Without the full story, I am prone to reach conclusions that are incongruent with reality. Perhaps this is the source of too much stress and anger in our daily lives: failing to believe the best and assuming the worst.

Which brings me back to the voice behind the Pillsbury Doughboy. The day finally arrived for our guest lecturer's visit, and I was blown away. My assumptions did not prepare me for the truth that the man behind the Pillsbury Doughboy looks nothing like the pastry-filled, giggling lump of animated dough I had imagined. The picture I had conjured up in my head failed in the light of reality!

That day, I met a distinguished gentleman named Cerby who greeted us with genuine warmth. Turns out Cerby has taken his earnings and wealth from over the years and leveraged his Pillsbury fortune to help others further their dreams in the streets of Chicago.

Cerby is smart, generous, jolly guy! He was nothing like what I had assumed in my imagination. Turns out that believing the best is a better default than assuming the worst.

BUYING PANTYHOSE AT 3 AM

One Saturday night while working at the comedy theater, I received a phone call that I was being activated as an understudy for a children's theater performance the next day. Somebody in the cast of the production was sick and so my moment in the spotlight was beckoning. I was excited until I realized that the production involved dressing up as a pirate and I needed to provide my own pantyhose. Apparently Captain Hook had an inner diva.

Pantyhose, really? I'm a guy which means I have an allergy to Haines and don't know the first thing about choosing pantyhose. But here I was after working the late shift at Second City, clumsily fumbling through the pantyhose aisle of a Walgreens at 3 am. I think my Man Card was suspended for the night.

Luckily, two women walked into the Walgreens and came to my aid: Rachel Dratch and Tina Fey. I shared earlier about how at this time in her life, Tina Fey was not big into parties after late night performances at Second City. Her regular rituals included renting movies at the local Blockbuster Video and grabbing a snack at the Walgreens across the street. This is how she and Dratch found me.

I wish I could say it was one of my finer moments in life but there's no way to spin it: I was a young college dude looking pathetic buying women's pantyhose.

Tina and Rachel must have thought I was nuts and easily could have assumed the worst about me and walked away. Instead they walked toward me. Instead of talking about me, they chose to talk with me. It didn't hurt that they recognized me from Second City, so they came over to ask what I was up to.

After I explained my predicament in a way that only professional theater people can understand, Tina took a few minutes to choose just the right color and size of pantyhose for me to dress up in as a pirate the next day.

Yes, it's true: Tina Fey helped me pick out pantyhose.

Actually purchasing the pantyhose was embarrassing. There is just no cool way for a twenty-year-old dude at 3 am to slyly hand over a pink package of *Haines Hosiery Thigh-Highs* and declare with security in their own manhood, "It's just something for the little lady at home."

Yes, I may have looked odd or even a bit creepy from the outside looking in. The cashier didn't crack a smile once during the checkout process, he just stared at me in judgment. And I can't blame him for assuming the worst about me. But isn't that how we all react when we encounter something out of the ordinary without all the information on the situation? What if we chose to believe the best about the people we encounter? What if we eclipsed our inner judge with a presumption of compassion?

At Life Church Michigan, we are willing to try anything and do anything short of sin to engage people who normally will not darken a church door. Having a whatever it takes attitude to reaching people far from God has led us on some wild adventures.

One idea that has gained traction and successfully reached families in our region each year is our annual Easter Egg Helicopter Drop. We invite folks to our church campus, throw a free party (remember, Jesus loved a good party!), and after they realize we are normal and harmless, we invite them back the next day for Easter services. We have heard story after story of people becoming Christ-followers as a direct result of our Egg Drop!

As you can imagine, when you throw 50,000 eggs out of a helicopter, the media takes notice. Flying plastic eggs play well for local news cameras. One year our Egg Drop even caught the attention of newspapers throughout Michigan and *The Christian Post*, a national online publication. People far from God loved our heart and passion for serving area families. However, the online comments sections were filled with venom and judgment . . . *from other Christians.*

As I read the first few comments from self-professing Christians, I felt like a hemophiliac in a razor factory. Instead of talking *to* us, brothers and sisters in Christ were talking *about* us on a public forum with assumptions that were not true. The statements made about our church's motives by people outside our church who claimed to represent the one true Church made people who go to church look stupid.

Assuming the worst can lead to unnecessary black-eyes within the Body of Christ. Friendly-fire is preventable. God gave us one mouth and two ears for a reason. It is always wiser to listen more than we speak.

Labeling people in public forums is not a sign of maturity—it's a preschool mentality. If we are unable to gather all the facts, then our default as Christ-followers needs to be believing the best about people, not assuming the worst.

We have a fantastic team of Interns at Life Church who are learning and growing in their leadership skills. Part of the program is that we are intentionally providing a safe environment to make mistakes in. We learn when we try.

When an intern makes a mistake in our church, we always believe the best. We walk alongside them, tell them to take a deep breath, and then we ask, "You're okay, you tried something new, now what did you learn from that experience?"

Believing the best can be a game changer in your life and your leadership. Jumping to positive conclusions creates energy, trust, and forward movement in any ensemble. Believing the best helps eliminate gossip and unnecessary drama.

Believe the best about the people you are partnering with and watch how your leadership climate shifts toward a stronger ensemble!

DON'T THROW A TEAMMATE UNDER AN ONCOMING BUS... SPLATTER TOGETHER!

> "Now will saying 'Yes' get you in trouble at times? Will saying 'Yes' lead you to doing some foolish things? Yes it will. But don't be afraid to be a fool." - Stephen Colbert

Comedy and leadership will both take you on wild adventures with risks hiding behind every corner. When you cannonball into the water, beneath the exhilaration of freedom lies dark undercurrents of fear. Thinking ensemble ensures you both endure together.

If you see a potential problem headed for your partner, give them a heads up! Nobody enjoys a blindside and becoming roadkill hurts. Comedians and leaders who see a bus coming full speed toward their teammates and give advance warning are cool, but if you are willing to actually jump out front and become roadkill yourself, you rise to the rare level of Truly Awesome. And honestly, isn't that the level we all aspire for?

Self-preservation isn't celebrated by the media. Nobody remembers the name of the guy who threw his friends under an oncoming bus. If for some reason they do, they remember his name combined with a curse word.

Being willing to sound the alarm and link arms in the face of doom creates bonds of integrity and honor. Trust is the currency of today's world. People on your team will be inspired when you reject throwing someone under the bus and instead courageously splatter together.

The comedian or leader who is willing to take a bullet for their teammate earns that teammate's respect and trust for life. When you are willing to link arms and go through hell together, the bond becomes stronger and the journey more exciting based on the shared experience.

Trust is critical to making things happen. If you want to do awesome things, you have to be known as an awesome partner. In short, always support your teammates and think ensemble. It will move the ball forward relationally and lead toward delightful discoveries together.

SUPPORT YOURSELF

"It will never be perfect, but perfect is overrated. Perfect is boring on live TV." - Tina Fey

Africa is hot in July. Serving in the villages and slums of Zambia over the course of a couple summers, my wife and I were ready to spend our final day overseas exploring the African Bush. This meant getting up earlier than the sun to join our Safari group in an open-air jeep.

Our tour guide, Majimbo, was a quiet man with deep knowledge of African wildlife. We pushed off into the wild through the early morning mist, brimming with excitement of what we might discover. We encountered wild turkeys, giraffes, and warthogs that comically run with their fannies in the air.

Midway through our journey, Majimbo slowed the jeep down as a discreet hush fell over our hearty crew. Slowly, Majimbo gingerly reached for a weapon previously hidden under his seat: a large gun. This sobered our crew in a hurry.

Then in the distance, we saw him: an African rhino. He seemed to be far off and deep in rhino thoughts. After several minutes of intense silence, I leaned toward Majimbo and whispered, "What's up?" Majimbo turned slightly toward me, never breaking gaze with the rhino, and whispered back in African clicks: "Click-click Clack-moowah!"

Nah, I'm kidding with you! He said, "Behold, the Rhino." Turns out that wild rhinos are among the most dangerous land animals in Africa. When startled or threatened, a wild rhino will run top-speed toward his target, his dangerous horn directed toward his prey. Once he begins his charge, there is no stopping him. This makes the rhino an unstoppable force.

The funny thing about rhinos is that they are near-sighted; they can only see a few feet in front of themselves clearly. Beyond that limited range of vision, everything is blurry and out of focus. Rhinos are unstoppable forces that move forward not by sight, but by faith!

Scientists have observed that six weeks out of every year, rhinos will come together to form a pack for mating purposes. If you should encounter this group and cause them to charge, there's a scientific name for this unstoppable force of nature: a Crash.

I love this! Rhinos are the perfect allegory for the Church: both are created to be a powerful ensemble that when focused becomes an unstoppable force, moving forward by faith, occasionally crashing into things! A church focused on its mission will take ground and expand its reach, just like these wild beasts of Africa. Rhinos united during that small window of opportunity are a Crash, but it starts with a solo rhino taking a stand and supporting himself.

PRAYED UP, PREPPED UP, PUNCTUAL

"If the first thought in your head when you approach an improv scene is 'Support your partner'... what are you supporting them with? Are you supporting them with thoughts about supporting them? That's very nice but not very supportive.... Do you say nice things to them, do you uber-agree, do you pat them on the head, offer them a chair, rub their shoulders? No, the most supportive thing you can do is get over your pasty self and selfishly make a strong choice in the scene. Then you are supporting your partner with your power, and not your fear. If you want to support your partner in an improv scene, give them the gift of your choice."
- Mick Napier

Mick was one of my improvisational comedy teachers. Along with developing television ideas for Comedy Central and founding The Annoyance Theater in Chicago, Mick is a premiere professor of improv and Second City's go-to director for main-stage productions. Mick has directed improvisers ranging from Tina Fey to Stephen Colbert. Completely humble with a Joker-like smile, Mick has a different take on how comedy works that I've always appreciated.

Mick was the first to propose a new foundational-yet-advanced rule for beginning a comedy scene: Support Yourself. While it seems to grate against thinking ensemble, supporting yourself simply means going into every scene with an activity, emotion, or strong statement.

Taking care of yourself first sets everyone up by:

1. Getting things going faster

2. Providing instant information your partner can use

3. Giving you something to do that makes the audience comfortable.

What do I mean by comfortable? If the audience sees you standing there doing nothing, they think, "Oh no, he doesn't know what to do. He's worried. He's confused."

Then they feel bad. The audience wants the comic to succeed. The moment you launch into an activity (baking bread, counting money, sweeping the floor) or an emotion (hope, love, pride), the audience thinks, "Oh, I see. He knows what's going on. He has a plan," and then they relax and enjoy the show.

Of course, you don't really have a plan, and you don't really know what's going on.

Mick Napier once said to me, "Improvisation is the art of being completely okay with not knowing what you're doing." The dirty little secret is that the best improvisers appear completely confident even when they have no idea what's going on.

This applies to leadership as well. When you're the leader, everyone is watching you, gauging your reactions, and feeding off your emotion and energy. You reflect what your organization will become. You become the unstoppable force. And let's be honest, church world is really one big act of improvisation complete with the unplanned, the unexpected, and daily gray zones.

Remember the Easter Egg Helicopter Drop I mentioned earlier? This annual outreach involves so many people that it could easily become an overwhelming logistical nightmare. This type of event requires a large spending budget and massive volunteer support. Hours and hours are spent planning, creating buy-in with the business community, rallying skeptical volunteers to jump on board, and massively advertising the event throughout the region.

This past year, cashing in so many of my leadership poker chips for this single event made me a little queasy, to be honest. But as the leader, I walked into that big day ready to inspire and cheerlead. I could only take care of leading my people after I had taken care of myself first.

I arrived that day walking in the security of who I am in Christ, confidently calling the shots and helping our volunteers serve their hearts out. We saw thousands of people descend upon our campus and even created a traffic jam on the main drag!

Everything went off without a hitch, and we created a memory for our volunteers and a strong connecting point with families in our region. The result was seeing over fifty guests receive Christ into their lives the following day . . . all because they felt welcomed onto our church campus through a fun outreach event.

How did I prepare myself? Bill Hybels once said that a leader has to do whatever it takes and spare no expense to get ready. I prepare using the three P's:

Prayed Up

Like Jesus, I need to get away by myself to pray. This is hard with young children and so I highly recommend finding a closet or nature trail so that it's just you and the Father.

Prepped Up

Comedian Jim Breuer (*SNL*'s "Goat Boy") once shared with me that before every show he prepares by drinking a coffee, texting his wife, and spending a good half hour in silence. That's now my pre-game routine.

Punctual

If you're not five minutes early, you're late.

Everything rises and falls on leadership. Before you can lead others, you have to Support Yourself.

Your personal vibes will cause ripples, either positively or negatively. If you carry a lot of stress on your shoulders, fear will rub off and multiply among your team members. If you are secure in who you are and what God is calling you to do, people will rally behind your vision and be inspired to attempt great things. If your people know that you are walking solidly with the Lord, they will follow you through the fire.

MAKE STATEMENTS

When you're creating comedy on the fly, there is power in making statements. Don't respond to initiations with questions. Whatever the problem, be part of the solution.

Making statements is a positive way of saying: "Don't ask questions all the time." Don't just sit around raising hypothetical questions and pointing out obstacles. We've all worked with that person. That person is a deacon.

Instead of saying, "Where are we?" make a statement like, "We have arrived in the zoo, Cousin Jeb." There is power and clarity when you make a statement. Whoever speaks with the most clarity about the future gets to be leader.

Take a risk and make a statement. Believe me, people are not risk-averse; they are ambiguous-averse. Ambiguity doesn't empower; ambiguity deflates. You create clarity in whatever situation you face when you make statements.

Statements don't have to be over-analyzed. Just do it. Say it. Initiate something—anything—because everyone is waiting on you, and decision paralysis doesn't inspire anyone. Make statements.

QUESTIONS PARALYZE

Malcolm Gladwell is one of my favorite authors and speakers. He unashamedly wears his hair up in a funky style, shares a biting wit, and his grandfather was a Christian pastor. He also happens to have written two *New York Times* bestsellers.

Malcolm Gladwell's *Blink* focuses on how leaders make decisions in a split-second. Gladwell deftly makes the case that agonizing over leadership decisions actually complicates your brain, resulting in you making the wrong decision.

According to Gladwell's findings, leaders must come to a place where they can embrace "thin-slicing"—the ability to determine what is really important from a very narrow period of experience.

Thin-slicing happens in many professions where bold, decisive leadership is required. When critically-wounded patients are rushed to a trauma center, the surgeons must thin-slice by making split-second, life-saving decisions based on a narrow amount of information about each patient. There's little time for asking questions and decisive choices must be made.

Research shows that doctors who test and test and test to verify their initial gut hypothesis become paralyzed by asking more questions when the answer was already known in their first assessment. We overestimate the value of extra information. Every study shows that accuracy does not improve; only confidence improves.

Asking questions can stall forward movement when thin-slicing is the answer. And when the clock is ticking, prolonging treatment can prove deadly for some patients.

Now some of you may object. "But, Jon, (there's that 'but' again!), you said earlier that asking questions can improve my confidence!" True. However overconfidence can be deadly.

Overconfidence can lead to miscalibration (ignoring reality) by leaders who think they know more than they know. Examples include the Iraq War planning in 2002. Overconfidence can also lead to assumptions that trap us by our own confidence. Just look at what financial experts were saying pre-2008.

Let me give you a real-world example of how making statements works in church-world. One day I was wrestling with a significant leadership decision in our church and seeking wisdom and advice from everyone who had a pulse.

When I brought my dilemma to one of my ministry mentors, Perry Noble, he listened to me politely and then gave me this awesome advice:

> "Jonathan, you already know *what you need to do*."

Perry was right. I already knew the answer; I was just delaying to gain validation and self-confidence. Thinking up more questions was just a delay tactic. Thin-slicing already provided the correct answer.

WHEN YOUR HEAD FEELS LIKE A PIÑATA

In creating improvisational comedy, supporting yourself as you "think ensemble" unleashes confidence that frees the comedian to move the scene forward. For Christian leaders navigating through the minefields of life, we also want to see people moving their lives forward.

Yes, there is a time and a place for leaders to ask questions. Questions clarify, stretch, and probe. But when it comes time to make leadership decisions, questions can become your enemy.

Whether it's a comedy set or a church meeting, you have no script. All of life is one big improvisation. Actors and leaders are both on a live stage going with their gut—an exhilarating freedom. Sometimes it feels like your head is a piñata, other times it's like Flintstone vitamins to a child—pure delight.

Asking questions stalls action and kills momentum. It puts people in their heads, slowing down your partners and causing you to over-analyze the situation. (If you would just Yes, And, the scene/life would move forward!) Nine times out of ten, the correct answer is already within you; you just need to gather up the guts to courageously spit it out.

Time and again in church world, questions can become the coward's way of abdicating responsibility. An example:

PERSON 1: *"That is one huge clown balloon coming our way!"*

PERSON 2: *"Why is there a clown balloon on this hot, sunny day?"*

PERSON 1: *(sweating under stress)* *"Um . . . er . . . that rhymes!"*

PERSON 2: *"What?!"*

Sometimes we use questions as self-doubt or to pull the power out of an idea/statement: "I don't know, but . . ."

Don't apologize; declare! Create a judgment-free environment—a *Holy Shift* is built on trust and declarations. Decision paralysis is just another term for mediocrity. Fight it by making statements! In summary:

- Asking questions places an unneeded burden on your partner while making statements accepts their gift and heightens the moment.

- Asking questions can cause you to get stuck in your head while making statements releases and empowers you to move things forward.

- Asking questions doesn't make the funny while making statements makes the funny.

- Asking questions kills momentum while making statements unleashes potential.

USING QUESTIONS TO MAKE A STATEMENT

Now allow me to add a layer to what we just learned about questions. You can actually pull a ninja move and use a question to make a statement. The nice thing about statements is that they provide information you and your partner can immediately start building upon.

Why go through this:

> PERSON 1: "What time is it?"
>
> PERSON 2: "Uh, 3:30."
>
> PERSON 1: "Are you ready?"
>
> PERSON 2: "Yeah, are you ready?"
>
> PERSON 1: "What are we doing?"
>
> PERSON 2: "I don't know. What's the capital of South Dakota?"
>
> PERSON 1: "Uh, Fargo?"

When you could have:

> PERSON 1: "It's 3:30."
>
> PERSON 2: "We're right on schedule."
>
> PERSON 1: "Johnson should be handing the teller the note right now."
>
> PERSON 2: "It's 3:31. Ski masks on."
>
> PERSON 1: "Think I have time to run to the bathroom?"
>
> PERSON 2: "Why don't I ever get paired with Johnson?"

Questions which don't require answers are fine. Questions which provide more information then they demand are gold: "Think I have time to run to the bathroom?" This question introduces information, raises the stakes, and doesn't require their partner to come up with a response. Rhetorical questions can be fun too: "Why don't I ever get paired with Johnson?"

PUT SOME CALCIUM IN YOUR SPINE

"You put all you dream about in jeopardy when you are indecisive. Nothing gets killed by your gun when all you say is, 'Ready, aim, aim, aim . . .'" - Dave Ramsey[7]

In church world, committees are notorious for delaying decisions by probing for additional information. A choice that should be made in five minutes can be stretched out to five months! Reject decision paralysis by making a statement toward action.

I remember one meeting where what should have been a five minute brief decision on the color of a wall turned into a two hour laborious drama! Do you think the Kingdom of God was being advanced during those two hours of debating the merits of "bright white" versus "eggshell white?" If I had a flying DeLorean and could go back in time, I would put some calcium in my spine, throw down the first color swatch in front of me, and declare: "This looks white enough to me. What's next?"

It's completely biblical to be forceful like a rhino. Jesus said, "From the days of John the Baptist until now, the kingdom of heaven has been forcefully advancing, and forceful men lay hold of it" (Matthew 11:12). There is Red Bull in that verse!

As the leader, your role is to be the calcium in the spine. Movements move. You have to make a move or you won't move.

Allow me to recall the story of rhinos in Africa that we talked about earlier. Fast-moving packs of rhinos are literally called a Crash—and that's what they're supposed to do! If rhinos aren't crashing, they aren't fulfilling what they were created for. I believe the same is true for churches.

When there are oxen in the barns, the barns are messy (see Proverbs 14:4). If you are moving your church forward, you will be crashing into walls and making lots of big messes! But you know what? I would rather have a packed and messy church than a clean and empty one.

If God is telling you to do something for Him, what worries could you possibly have? I'd be more worried about disobeying! If God can utterly conquer decay and destruction, and He is the One telling you to take this courageous step of faith, put all your chips on Him, not the phantom unknowns!

Reject momentary indecision paralysis; trust the Ancient of Days. Lead toward the cliff and then jump. Because that's what leaders do—they cannonball. And the people you are leading are waiting for you to jump first.

Gladwell's research would say that you already possess all the information you need to make the right choice. Trust the Spirit and stop asking questions as a cover. Make statements.

1. Define your reality. Leaders bring clarity to mist and fog.

2. Commit to your reality. Throw yourself into the mix full-speed.

Remember church leader, without FAITH, it is IMPOSSIBLE to please God:

"Remember who I am, and be content with My authority; for I have ready at hand ALL resources; when ANYTHING stands in your way, rely on My power, and EXECUTE what I commanded thee." - John Calvin on God

Not knowing where to begin is a common form of paralysis. Begin anywhere by supporting yourself, making a strong statement or choice and then discovering what happens with the ensemble. The compass is in your hands. Avoid fields and go jump some fences.

6

FAIL HARDER

One December evening the cry of "Fire!" echoed through Thomas Edison's plant. Spontaneous combustion had broken out in the film room and within moments all the packing compounds, film, and other flammable goods had gone up with a whoosh.

When the family couldn't find Edison, they became concerned. Was he safe? With all his assets going up in smoke, would his spirit be broken? He was 67, no age to begin anew.

Then they saw him in the plant yard, running toward the family.

"Where's Mom?" he shouted. "Go get her! Tell her to get her friends! They'll never see a fire like this again!"

At 5:30 the next morning, when the fire was barely under control, Thomas Edison called his employees together and announced: "We're rebuilding!" One man was told to lease all the machine shops in the area, another to obtain a wrecking crane from the Erie Railroad Company. Then, almost as an afterthought, he added, "Oh, by the way, anybody know where we can get some money?"

Later on he explained, "You can always make capital out of disaster. We've just cleared out a bunch of old rubbish! We'll build bigger and better on these ruins."

Just like live comedy, leadership in the local church means that you will face unexpected challenges. When you sign up to be a leader, you are never promised rainbows, Skittles, and unicorns. Navigating challenging seasons is key. That's why when you *Holy Shift*, there are no mistakes, only opportunities. I want to encourage you to fail harder!

YOU HAVE NO CHOICE BUT TO KEEP YOUR WINGS FLAPPING

Every time the Wright Brothers would attempt to fly their plane, they would bring enough extra materials for multiple crashes which means that every time they went out, they knew they would fail. They would crash and rebuild and crash and rebuild. That's why they eventually took off. If you dream big and work hard, you can do anything in this world.

Don't think outside the box; there is no box. Once you've done improv a bunch of times and failed, there's a freedom in the failure. It's like a free-fall in skydiving. Find something interesting that you couldn't have planned to find. Discovery is like Red Bull to a leader.

I shared about Martin de Maat earlier, one of my theater professors during my college years. Martin once surprised my wife Amber and me on a wintry Windy City evening with ice cream at a hole-in-the-wall diner, mixing his improvisational comedy philosophies with silly humor and engaging stories of Chicago lore. "You know," he whispered to us with a twinkle in his eye, "this booth we're sitting in right now is where The Beatles used to hang out after their shows!"

The effect Martin had in shaping my work as a communicator and leader is immeasurable. He always believed in taking big risks to discover new opportunities. In my old journal from his improv classes, I scratched out some of Martin's sayings that continue to guide me as a leader today:

> "You can get the biggest laugh in a scene simply by saying 'ahem.' It's all about context."

> "The Hokey Pokey. Think about it. At the end of the song, what do we learn? What is it all about? You put your whole self in!"

> "Always in life surround yourself with people who make you happy. Life is short and you will be surprised how much better your life is if you just stop hanging out with the jerks we are all drawn towards."

> "Do you have the right to call yourself an artist? The moment you manifested enough courage to enroll in your class you jumped off that cliff. You have no choice but to keep your wings flapping."

> "You have the right to follow your dreams. I'm giving you permission to follow your dreams."

FREE TO RISK

There are no mistakes, only opportunities. Even if an idea on a live stage completely bombs, it's a lesson on what does or does not connect with an audience. Failure also has the side effect of making you free to risk. The more your parachute fails, the thicker your skin gets for future falls.

Tina Fey once explained it this way:

> "The next big laugh is just around the corner as well as beautiful happy accidents. Many of the world's great discoveries have been an accident. Bad glue created sticky notes (Post-It® Notes). A bad test for a hypertension medication created the right medicine for erectile dysfunction (Viagra®). (Insert joke here.)
>
> "If I start a scene with what I think is very clearly a cop riding a bicycle, but you think I am a hamster in a hamster wheel, guess what? Now I'm a hamster in a hamster wheel. I'm not going to stop everything to explain that it was really supposed to be a bike . . . in improv, there are no mistakes, only beautiful happy accidents. And many of the world's greatest discoveries have been by accident. I mean, look at the Reese's Peanut Butter Cup or Botox."[8]

You may be thinking, "Okay Jon, how does this connect with leading a church?" I'm pressing you to go all out in reaching the lost at any cost. Author Craig Groeschel always says, "If you want to reach the people no one else is reaching, you have to do the things no one else is doing!" This means you will take risks, reap the rewards of lost people becoming found, and reap tons of criticisms and misunderstandings . . . from other Christians.

Understand that I am perfectly fine with reaching the lost at any cost. Hell is too hot and forever is too long for the local church to not ignite a rescue mission. That's what Jesus was all about—helping the sick, not the healthy. (He enlisted the healthy to open more hospitals: church plants.)

A long time ago in a galaxy far, far away, I had the privilege of serving as the youth pastor at NewSpring Church in Anderson, South Carolina, which is one of the fastest growing churches in North America. I loved serving under the leadership of Perry Noble and learned a ton from him. He continues to be a mentor and strong influence in my life today.

What I found intoxicating at NewSpring as a leader were the risks we were free to make. Innovation was encouraged and new solutions were constantly being discovered for reaching lost people. One team brainstorming session revolved around how to amplify a teaching on the depth and meaning of worshiping God. An idea arose to set-up an environment during a Sunday morning service where the crowd believed that country music superstar Tim McGraw was going to make a surprise appearance.

A limo was parked outside the church doors and Perry shared an elaborate story of meeting McGraw the day before at a nearby restaurant and inviting him to church. This perfectly set up the crowd for McGraw to make an impromptu appearance. Everyone rose to their feet cheering and expecting to see Tim McGraw walk-out on stage. Tim McGraw did not come out because he wasn't really there; it was all a ruse.

Perry seized that moment to pound home the simple truth that they were worshiping: ascribing worth to someone outside one's self with passionate focus is the essence of what worship truly is. Was it risky to pull a bait-and-switch in the middle of a sermon? You bet, but the gamble paid off with an impacting message that people still talk about eight years later.

DON'T THINK OUTSIDE THE BOX

> "Surprise your audience for laughs. Surprise comes from the unexpected. Get there by bringing in 'crazy.' Don't think in a straight line. No one laughs because a scene makes sense."
> - Mick Napier[9]

Being willing to fail harder allows you to smash expectations as you bend self-made boundaries. What were once thought of as mistakes now become opportunities for discovery.

For example, how many times during the summer months do you drive by a church building with a big colorful sign out front advertising their week-long Vacation Bible School program? At one time in the past, VBS was an innovative, outside-the-box experiment in reaching children far from God. The first VBS was held in Hopedale, Illinois in 1894 and it worked! VBS caught on like wildfire among churches nationwide precisely because church leaders discovered it was a great opportunity for serving the community.

Fast-forward 100+ years and it seems like everyone and their grandma does VBS. I'm confident VBS can still reach kids for the gospel, but more often than not it is also treated as glorified babysitting for busy parents. Instead of the hosting church making lasting in-roads into the life of a new family, the parents just enroll their kids into the next VBS down the street and the next and the next, hopping from church to church for short-time childcare purposes, not long-term spiritual harvesting.

What if we took the heart and passion behind Vacation Bible School and applied it in our churches year-round? Think about it: your church volunteers rally behind the vision for a week of impact. Why not take it to another level and cast vision for that same level of quality and excitement every single Sunday during the year? How many more families might your church reach by taking a risk, stretching the team to invest in a long-term endeavor, and cannonballing into the deep end of the pool?

Would such an idea be perfect right out the gate? No, but that's ok! Go beyond thinking outside the box! The only way you're going to learn is by punching holes through cardboard. Don't think outside the box; obliterate the box! Don't just push the envelope; shred it! Take a risk by telling your team that this will be an experiment. If it succeeds, celebrate! If it fails, throw your hands in the air and declare, "That's ok; it was just an experiment!" Learn from what didn't work so that you'll be better in the future.

WHEN RISKS GET YOU FIRED

"I didn't see it then, but it turned out that getting fired from Apple was the best thing that could have happened to me. The heaviness of being successful was replaced by the lightness of being a beginner again, less sure about everything. It freed me to enter one of the most creative periods of my life." - Steve Jobs[10]

We've all seen the success stories of leaders who risked it all and then have seen God bless their efforts. But what about the stories of leaders who take a risk and it doesn't end well? Allow me to share how I once got fired.

We were going all out in reaching people far from God: throwing Easter eggs out of flying helicopters, covering current songs by groups like Foo Fighters and Beyonce that tied in with strong gospel messages, yelling at men to man up, etc. The fruit of our ministry was fantastic! In less than two years, we saw 328 professions of faith and 135 public baptisms all in a town of less than 5,000 people.

The life-change was awesome. Marriages were being healed, teenagers were getting fired up in their faith, and as a church we were aggressively paying off debt accumulated by the previous senior pastor. Other church leaders throughout our region were even coming to see what God was doing in our midst.

Then it suddenly came to an abrupt stop. As it turns out, our cutting-edge ministry techniques were being misunderstood by a very small but vocal pocket of hard-core traditionalists ("We love Jesus and we're *ANGRY* about it!"). They didn't like all the new people coming in with tattoos and leaving cigarette butts in the parking lot.

Since I was the senior pastor, I became their secret target. It was a shadow campaign of whispers and character slander as the ugly face of insider church politics quietly took root.

Forget Matthew 18; without my knowledge they leapfrogged straight to the executive pastor and church board with an ultimatum: "Him or Us." With a newly-hired, inexperienced executive pastor who had his eye on the top job, swaying the board became easy.

I was abruptly tossed out.

Did I mention that this leadership coup happened while I was at home on medical leave recovering from two back surgeries?

Adding insult to injury, the executive pastor and head of the church board both instructed church staff to completely cut-off all contact with me and my family. When the worship pastor reached out to me, they shamed him into thinking he was somehow personally responsible for all this happening. The board publicly announced that I had chosen to resign my position when that could not have been further from the truth.

Out of nowhere, my life became a real-life country song: I lost my health, I lost my job, and our closest friends and small group all bailed on us . . . I felt like I was reenacting the Book of Job. The stress even gave me boils like Job. It was awesome.

This was the most painful season our family had ever experienced as we were faced with deep betrayal, widespread gossip, and the Amish weapon-of-choice: shunning. If you've been in ministry for any length of time, you will understand: ministry hurts. Hurting people hurt people. Sheep bite.

The Bible is true when it reminds us that a prophet is not honored in his hometown. You will be misunderstood, misperceived, and mishandled. Even Jesus had a Judas.

God, however, is not surprised by the junk that happens in your life. Jesus said, "In this world you will have trouble." Nice. Thank God (literally!) that Jesus followed that statement up with, "But take heart for I have overcome the world!" Turns out, God is supremely in charge. He really does know what He's doing, and He never wastes a hurt.

These words from the Amplified Version of the Bible spoke to my heart during this season of life. I wrote them out and posted them on my bathroom mirror as a daily reminder that there are no mistakes, only opportunities:

> *"For God Himself has said, 'I will not in any way fail you nor give you up nor leave you without support.*

> *I will not, I will not, I will not in any degree leave you helpless nor forsake you nor let you down (relax My hold on you) . . .*
>
> *The LORD is my Helper; I will not be seized with alarm (I will not fear or dread or be terrified).*
>
> *What can man do to me?"* - Hebrews 13:5-6 (AMP)

I don't know where you fall on the theological spectrum, but I camp out in the tribe that trusts God is completely and intricately in charge of all things. Resting in the sovereignty of God isn't just my theology, it's my sanity.

There are no mistakes in God's sheet music. If the Lord is orchestrating the music, I can enjoy my time banging around on my drum set.

At the risk of over-simplifying our story, God took a church board's mistake and made it an awesome opportunity for our family. Yes, it was very painful and hard to walk through at the time. People we had loved and trusted said and did some very painful things to our family.

That's why the Bible says over and over again these prophetic words: "And it came to pass."

Whatever it is, it will pass. Going through a rough season? Don't worry. It will pass. Experiencing an awesome year? Drink it up, because it will pass! Facing a tough illness? Either it will pass or you will pass; either way Jesus is with you!

There is always a purpose behind your pain and at some point, it will pass. What I learned through this trial was to make a *Holy Shift* in my thinking and understand that it's not a mistake; it's an opportunity.

LEARNING TO RISK AGAIN

"You can walk through the valley of the shadow of death, but don't build a house there." - Martin de Maat

A year after everything collapsed in our lives, we found ourselves in a healthy and fruitful season. The biggest joy was expanding our family by adopting a precious baby girl, Ainsleigh Grace. When your family is touched by the blessing of adoption, you are offered a deeper understanding of God's grace which adopts us (Ephesians 1).

Through a careful and lengthy process, my wife and I discerned that God was telling us to bloom where He had planted us. It would have been much easier to pick up and move away; it is harder to stay and remain.

With the advice of wise counsel, we launched a new church located 45 minutes away in the heart of the nation's murder capital, Saginaw, Michigan. As if these blessings weren't enough, it was during this season that I received an unsolicited book contract that led to my first book. You see, there always has to be a death before there can be a resurrection.

Studies show that entrepreneurial leaders average 3.8 failures before final success. What sets the successful ones apart is their amazing persistence. There are no mistakes, only opportunities, so go fail harder!

For us, one church board's clumsy mistake became a fresh opportunity to dream again as a beginner with a fresh canvas. God gave our family time to paint a picture of the future. Following Christ doesn't make life risk free; it means you can walk away from mediocrity and become free to risk.

Every new twist in life always reminds me of these words from Heraclitus of Ephesus:

> "No man steps into the same river twice, for it is not the same river and he is not the same man."

Our family has tried many times over the years to personally reach out and engage with the people who were involved in this painful leadership coup. Every time we've stuck our neck out to initiate, our authenticity has been greeted with silence and rejection. And so we continue to pray for them, asking God to use their ministry in mighty ways, and for gospel-centered reconciliation to occur.

I carefully weighed out if and how to share this personal story in these pages. At the end of the day, God's Spirit spoke to me that sharing would serve as an encouragement to all the ministry leaders out there who have or who will experience getting fired for taking risks. You are not alone and there are no mistakes, only opportunities.

Would you like to know what happened to my former worship pastor who had dared to reach out to us during that dark season? He and almost the entire rest of the pastoral staff left within ten months. He slowly and carefully worked through some of the hurts he personally experienced during that same period. At one point he strongly considered leaving ministry altogether and he actually earned his commercial trucker driver license!

Three years later, by God's grace, he entered a very healthy season of life . . . and ended up on-staff at our new start-up at Life Church!

Did bringing him on our team require some tough, raw, heart-to-heart conversations? Absolutely. Were either of us comfortable as we relived old conversations and humbly apologized for choices made in the mistakes? No, we were not comfortable, but it was the right thing to do.

God's response to sin is never shaming, gossiping, shunning, or nagging. God's response to sin is grace.

Do you know what makes the world take notice? When brothers in Christ reconcile and forgive each other. The world watches when Christians walk toward people, not away. The world is compelled when Christians talk to people, not about people.

In the grand scheme of things, there are no mistakes, only opportunities. And sometimes that opportunity is an invitation to reconcile and grow as a disciple in grace.

FREE YOUR TEAM TO FAIL HARDER

As Facebook exploded, founder Mark Zuckerberg realized he had to release more and more of the work to web programmer and developers. He couldn't do it all by himself.

Sometimes details fell through the cracks. Mistakes happened. And that's okay. Zuckerberg knew that effective leaders cannot micromanage people. You must give them freedom and margin to hit the wall and learn.

Fail Harder. That's his mantra at Facebook. Move fast and break things. The same is true for you: your effectiveness as a leader will INCREASE as the load on your plate DECREASES. For church leaders, this means enabling more and more people.

Life Church is one of the fastest-growing churches in Michigan. As the founding pastor, my temptation is to try doing everything. This temptation is why the super-majority of churches never grow beyond 200 people!

What I have been learning as we bust through growth barriers is that as the leader I can have either control or growth, but I can't have both. When I let go of control, our church experiences more growth!

I believe in the saying, "Saved People Serve People." But remember, as you release ministry, you unleash mistakes. And that's okay. Comedians get better and better every time they bomb on stage. There is no better teacher than a mistake.

Wisdom is simply knowledge plus scars. We cannot microwave leaders. You have to give your workers time to make mistakes. Crockpots cook s-l-o-w-l-y.

Thomas Edison famously said, "I have not failed. I've just found 10,000 ways that won't work." Failure is the incubator of leadership. Failure says that we get to try another direction in solving this problem. Leadership is formed when we choose to fail harder.

Whatever happened before is now in the past. Following Christ is like an improv scene: you always get to start fresh. Dream big. Stand back up and stretch your faith further. That's the beauty of following Christ. Your vision is never too big for God. He forgives, He authors second acts, and He releases you from your past (see Romans 8:1).

Now be careful; don't waste this fresh page. Don't be obligated to ordinary. No one will ever follow you down the street if you're carrying a banner that says, "Onward toward mediocrity."

Instead, take risks. Paint a big picture of what could be and should be.

And then do it.

7

BE COMPLETELY UNAFRAID TO DIE

"The enemy is fear. We think it is hate. But, it is fear." - Gandhi

My heart is in Africa.

Spending a couple summers in the African villages of northern Zambia, serving orphans, spreading the gospel to thousands, and helping plant a church in Lusaka changed me. My heart was filled with a greater awareness, compassion, and brokenness for the world.

The teenagers with us felt the same way. We had brought along high schoolers from our church's student ministry for the journey. Turns out that teens need an outlet for over-brimming emotional experiences in Africa.

So, they went bungee jumping.

And it wasn't just any old bungee jump; it was the world's highest. Did I forget to mention that the group was taking turns bungee jumping over the world's longest waterfall at the base of the Zambezi River?

Some people would call this the definition of insanity; the teens would call it an excellent time to haze Jon. They tried and tried and tried to get me to bungee jump, but I refused. There was just something about the complete lack of safety equipment in a third world country surrounded by silly grins on the bungee operators' faces that turned me off.

Side note: In early 2012, a story made the international news that a female jumper's bungee snapped while she was falling, hurtling her into croc-infested waters. Can you guess where this happened (grin)?

Now, ignore that side note so I can make my point. I missed a once-in-a-lifetime opportunity because I refused to jump. My fear eclipsed my sense of adventure. And that is precisely what separates the amateurs from the greats.

BILL MURRAY'S BEST ADVICE EVER

The credo in improvisational comedy that sums up this principle is to commit fully to whatever you are doing. Half-hearted will not do; only the lion-hearted are remembered. If you can crash through your fears, you will be in a position to drink fully from the hose of life.

Bill Murray, one of Second City's most famous alumni, cannonballs on screen and in life. He learned to cannonball while practicing live comedy on stage:

> "(You gotta) commit. Don't walk out there with one hand in your pocket unless there's somethin' in there you're going to bring out.
>
> "You gotta commit. You've gotta go out there and improvise and you've gotta be completely unafraid to die. You've got to be able to take a chance to die. And you have to die lots. You have to die all the time.

"You're goin' out there with just a whisper of an idea. The fear will make you clench up. That's the fear of dying.

"When you start and the first few lines don't grab and people are going like, 'What's this? I'm not laughing and I'm not interested,' then you just put your arms out like this and open way up and that allows your stuff to go out. Otherwise it's just stuck inside you." [11]

MAKE A BOLD CHOICE

"That you do something is far more important than what you do."
- Mick Napier

When you're moving forward without a road map, you must make a bold choice. When an improviser approaches the two empty chairs and bare stage to begin a scene from scratch, he must initiate with a bold choice. If it's wimpy and neutered, nothing is ignited.

What's true for improvisational comedy is true for leadership; nobody is inspired by mediocrity. Whether you're leading a church start-up or leading off an improv scene, the people around you are following your lead.

Leaders set the bar and guard the bar. Upset that your people aren't brimming with passion for your church's vision? Look in the mirror. Your people will only be as passionate as you are.

In the Old Testament when a king was crowned, the priest would elaborately pour flowing anointed oil over the new leader's head as a sign of God's hand upon him. The oil always drips from the beard. So goes the leader, so goes the people. If you lead without conviction and energy, don't be surprised in six months to have a ministry of mediocrity.

Don't just stick your toe into the water . . . Cannonball! Make a bold choice. Bold conviction leads to construction. And if the potential choice makes you perspire, let it rip toward others and inspire!

Every time I look at heroes in the Bible, I see leaders who have embraced a *Holy Shift* toward an "out there on the edge live or die" commitment to leadership. Nobody ever changed the world by playing it safe! You have to make a choice. Might as well make it bold!

NO FEAR

> "We want to see your power, not your fear. Nobody has time for your fear." - Mick Napier

Life is too short to be imprisoned by fears: fear of rejection, failure, embarrassment. These fears only hold back your true potential. Nobody has time for your fear, not even you.

I know a guy who wronged someone close to him and was too proud to reconcile that relationship. Whenever he was pressed about sucking it up and apologizing, his response was, "Well, it would be too awkward." Wow. Do you know what's truly awkward? Looking back at your life and realizing you were more committed to self-preservation than gospel-saturated reconciliation. Don't allow fear to dictate your life.

When you are creating comedy on the spot without a script, you also don't have time to pause, think about things, wish you had more props to play with, or think deeply about what your next line will be. Because the spotlight is hot, the audience is waiting, and crickets are death to comedians.

In improvisational comedy, you just do it. Take a risk. Jump. Paralysis kills forward movement. Nobody is inspired by hand wringing. Entrepreneurs like church planters and ministry pioneers have to get the hang of creating something out of nothing every day.

That's the essence of entrepreneurial leadership. Whether you're a writer for late-night comedy or a parachute church planter, you are essentially creating something out of nothing. With respect to God, it's *ex nihilo*.

You have no script to start from, only a clean sheet. You are constantly living out what exists only in your head. Convincing others to join in is part of the adventure.

If you don't believe the reality in which you're choosing to exist, nobody else will. You lead the way.

You must be totally sold-out without seeing the destination. There is tension there. Comedians have to fully commit to the reality they are creating in the moment. The same is true for church planters:

>   You don't have a budget.

>   You don't have a building.

>   You don't have a staff.

>   You don't have a fall-back.

In improv comedy, it's just you, two chairs, and an empty stage. In church planting, it's just you and two chairs. No stage yet.

Yet, out of that environment, the miracle occurs. Something is birthed where nothing once stood. The dream becomes the reality. People join in. And the story begins . . .

HEALTHY THINGS GROW

Don't get me wrong, doing God's work is hard work. But every time you cannonball into the pool, there's going to be waves. You might as well choose to enjoy being a kite in God's hurricane.

When you let go of the side of the pool and jump in fully trusting God, growth and life change occur. In fact, that's a credo I declare over our church time and time again: healthy things grow. If my 8-month-old daughter suddenly stopped growing, I'd take her to the doctor and ask what's wrong. Obviously, something isn't healthy. Does she need vitamins? Exercise? More *Blues Clues*?

The same is true of the Church. Healthy things grow. If forward progress is being made, we should see dynamic spiritual and numerical growth, right?

If the Church is not growing, we diagnose the problem with honesty, no-holds-barred. Nobody likes a diagnosis that dances around the issue. Like the physician, we put together a plan to nurture health that naturally stimulates growth.

YOU'RE NOT GUARANTEED ANOTHER SEASON

Does God laugh at our plans? I think so. Either we dream too small and He blows us out of the water, or we don't dream big enough, lacking the kind of faith that moves mountains and becoming paralyzed by the unknown.

We can either choose to jump into God's ocean with a faith-filled, cannonball-sized splash, or as Scripture reveals repeatedly, He'll just pass over us and wait to use the next generation for His purposes (see: Moses)!

I believe my vision is never too big for God. But He gets to set the agenda for the Church, not me. Jesus is the senior pastor, not me (1 Peter 5). I've got one life to live and I want to exhaust every breath and opportunity for Jesus.

On *SNL*, every cast member is a union actor/writer. Contracts are renegotiated annually. Sometimes Lorne Michaels keeps you for a few seasons; sometimes you're a one season blip. Everyone eventually bows out at some point. Even Don Pardo at age 90 retired from announcing *SNL* after 34 years. You are not guaranteed another season. So live it up now.

You do not control your destiny—God's eternal purposes converge with your desires in life. Enjoy this moment. Don't fret over what happens to your church after your gone. It's not even yours!

Love widely. Give generously (and maybe have a will leaving a tithe of your entire estate to your local church for God's work). And don't worry about your legacy. I think it was author Matt Chandler who once observed, "We maybe only get 40 years."

It doesn't matter right now who will be the next senior pastor or leader to follow you. Be the most faithful one you can be now. God's got the details . . . and the future.

Improv teacher Del Close once told this story:

> "I was reading in the newspaper about a skydiver who dived out of airplanes and did aerial acrobatics for several thousand feet.
>
> "When he pulled the ripcord, the main chute did not open.

> "And then what did he do? He did flips and acrobatics head over heels at the top of his ability all the way into the ground. Splat.
>
> "Now that's my kind of guy. That's a kind of metaphor for life, isn't it? I mean, we're all going to hit the ground—splat—eventually, aren't we? So what I'm going to do is follow that guy's example and do acrobatics all the way out."

Timidity is uninspiring and a waste of energy. Throw yourself into the water and create waves. Charles Spurgeon lamented that we try to preserve ourselves as fine specimens of mankind when we were created to exhaust our lives for advancing the cause of Christ. Exhaust yourself in reaching people far from God!

THE NEW GROUND FLOOR

When you make the *Holy Shift* in your leadership, you must remain a student of the past, but remember you cannot live there. Always remember that the previous generation's ceiling is your ground floor.

Make that your mantra as you cannonball into the unknown depths of the pool. Honor the past by forging the future. The world needs more leaders with a *Holy Shift* mentality, men and women with maverick hearts to join the cause and forge the unknown. We are all waiting on you! Remember: Don't just dip your toe into the water . . . Cannonball!

The Church of Jesus Christ continues to be a world-shaking movement that is constantly welcoming, always inclusive, continually growing. The white-hot passion for igniting such a movement in your region begins with you. Embrace a bold choice from your new ground floor. Make a *Holy Shift*.

"The great difference between present-day Christianity and that of which we read in these letters is that to us it is primarily a performance, to them it was a real experience. We are apt to reduce the Christian religion to a code, or at best a rule of heart and life. To these men it is quite plainly the invasion of their lives by a new quality of life altogether. They do not hesitate to describe this as Christ 'living in' them.

"There were no churches, no Sundays, no books about the Faith. Slavery, sexual immorality, cruelty, callousness to human suffering, and a low standard of public opinion, were universal; traveling and communications were chancy and perilous; most people were illiterate. Many Christians today talk about the 'difficulties of our times' as though we should have to wait for better ones before the Christian religion can take root. It is heartening to remember that this faith took root and flourished amazingly in conditions that would have killed anything less vital in a matter of weeks.

"These early Christians were on fire with the conviction that they had become, through Christ, literally sons of God; they were pioneers of a new humanity, founders of a new Kingdom. They still speak to us across the centuries. Perhaps if we believed what they believed, we might achieve what they achieved."
- J.B. Phillips, 1947[12]

SECTION THREE
ACCELERATE CHURCH GROWTH

8

COMEDY-DRIVEN SERMONS

Now we are going to pivot from ideas about using comedy techniques in church leadership and begin fleshing out practical, hands-on best practices for actually doing this, beginning with writing messages.

Preaching is the main event. In the course of a year, I know I will have 50 opportunities to speak vision and life over our people (I say 50 because we shut down on July 4th weekend and on the final Sunday of each year. Why? Because Life Church exists to reach people far from God and I promise you that lost people do not go to church those two weekends!).

In Romans 10, the Apostle Paul tells us:

> *And how are they to believe in him of whom they have never heard? And how are they to hear without someone preaching? . . . Faith comes from hearing, and hearing through the word of Christ.*

This is where comedians and pastors overlap in the most obvious way: no other professions entail facing a blank sheet of paper on Monday with the weekly personal grind of creating new material to deliver that weekend in front of a live audience.

In 2015, we initiated the following practical steps in this chapter at Life Church and saw God grow our church by 400+ people in less than 12 months. No joke. Here is the *Holy Shift* I took as the lead pastor of Life Church Michigan to think like a comedian and create Comedy-Driven Sermons.

HAVE A PLAN, WRITE IT DOWN

Every year I buy giant oversized Post-It writing pads to plaster on the walls. I list out all the Sundays for the coming year and begin planning out message series. I tend to stick to four to six week series for three reasons:

1. A twelve month line-by-line expository preaching series is great for insiders, but very difficult for outsiders. I do not believe that expository preaching is something to die on a hill for.

    For example, you do not see Jesus or Peter or Paul doing expository preaching in the Bible. It drives my Reformed friends nuts that Jesus taught toward felt needs.

    Now if your church is rocking expository AND reaching people far from God, more power to you. That's awesome. In the Great Lakes Bay Region where I serve, that approach would not fly. I'm a missionary and I understand my cultural context. We purposefully keep each series short to hold people's attention.

2. Shorter series create easier on-ramps for guests and newcomers. Plan on doing message series that last about

four to six weeks each so that you have a defined beginning, middle, and end.

3. Shorter series build natural momentum in the life of your church. When I can ramp up toward a new series every four to six weeks, it creates something fresh and new to grab the focus of folks on the periphery.

On the giant sticky pads, I flesh out the different series we will journey through for the year. Writing things down makes it more real and creates personal accountability for you. Having a written plan helps you focus and communicates to your church that you are purposefully shepherding the flock with a plan in mind. Clarity is always a win in leadership.

THINK SEASONS

As I'm fleshing out the year's message series, I alternate between two types of series: Red Bull messages and Chiropractics.

Red Bull messages feature fun themes that stick in people's minds with the goal of growing in width: reaching people far from God, firing the crowd up, calling people to repentance, and making heaven more crowded.

Some examples of Red Bull messages from Life Church include:

- *Bringing Sexy Back*
- *Who the [BLEEP] Did I Marry?*
- *Star Wars Christmas*

The stickier the big idea, the easier it is for your people to share the message series branding on Facebook, Twitter, and Instagram. Your message series can be a tool in the tool belt for reaching people far from God. We strategically launch new Red Bull series during the seasons that people are naturally open to trying out church:

- January: What naturally goes up every new year? Gym memberships and church attendance. Leverage that bump by giving your people something to talk about.

- Easter: If tons of visitors are already coming on Easter Sunday, what better time to launch a sticky series that will cause them to come back for more? In 2015 we launched a series on building stronger marriages because everyone deals with relationship struggles. Our church permanently grew by 200 people!

- Mothers Day: This is your last chance before summer hits to engage new people. This will also be your third-highest attended Sunday of the year.

- September: Parents are coming back from vacations and getting back into their routines and schedules. If your staff team is firing on all cylinders, you should see the number of people who came on Easter Sunday now coming every Sunday in September.

- December: Just like at Easter, people far from God are actually open and willing to give your church a shot. Why not leverage the season with a fun message branding that points people to hope in Christ?

Chiropractic messages focus on discipleship and making adjustments in our daily lives with the goal of growing in depth: creating hunger for God's Word, diving deeper into a practical subject matter, pointing to the supremacy of Christ in all things. Some examples of Chiropractic messages from Life Church.

- *Erasing Clark Kent (Growing into Biblical Manhood)*
- *Angry Birds (A Study of Pharisees)*
- *Follow Me (Jesus' Approach to Discipleship)*

We still aim for a creative branding in a Chiropractic series, yet the aim is more toward current Christ-followers seeking to go deeper. We strategically launch new Chiropractic series during the seasons that people are naturally away from regular church attendance.

- February and March: In Michigan, this is the darkest of winter. If people are plowing themselves out of their driveways to get to church on time, these die-hards are most likely not first time guests.

- Summer: There's a strange annual ritual in the High Five State as Michiganders "go up North" on the weekends. Being an Iowan, I always assumed that going up North meant swinging through Wisconsin.

  Turns out northern Michigan is beautiful in the summer and people go camping. I've never understood why you would pretend to be homeless for a week, so I stay home and preach.

  At Life Church, we unplug and move our services outdoors for an annual series we call, "Lawn Chair Sundays." It allows our people to do something different, rub shoulders in lawn chairs with folks they don't always sit by indoors, and enjoy the outdoors without going to that mysterious place I cannot find on Google Maps: Up North.

- October and November: This is another strategic season to dig into something meaty and build up your regular attenders in their walks with Christ.

PUTTING PEN TO PAPER

Now that I have Life Church's message themes planned out for the year on the macro level, I can dive into the micro details of nailing down each week's messages. On the jumbo pads, I list out the name/big idea of each week's message and include a key scripture passage. This empowers my worship pastor to plan creative elements and set lists weeks ahead of time. When you have a written plan months ahead of time, it reduces stress and enables long-range creative thinking.

With the year fleshed out, I can carve out time each week to work on upcoming messages. I'm in a good spot if I can be six weeks ahead on my messages. This allows plenty of time for praying, researching, editing, and memorizing everything. How do I come up with message material? I think like a comedian by avoiding information cocoons and reading widely.

AVOID INFORMATION COCOONS

When I was studying improvisational comedy at Second City in Chicago during the late 1990's, every night was a Master's Class on comedy as I observed a mainstage cast including Scott Adsit (*30 Rock*), Kevin Dorff (writer for *The Tonight Show, Conan*), and Tina Fey (*SNL, 30 Rock*).

I looked up to them while night after night they were consistently working "from the top of their intelligence." This is an expression used in comedy circles to differentiate between the comedians who go for the easy, dumb, expletive, sex jokes versus the comedians who work harder to create material that is thought-out, intelligent and not swearing like a pirate. You will always be better, funnier, and command more respect when you work from the top of your intelligence.

At the time, I was reading Gilda Radner's autobiography, *It's Always Something*, hoping to glean some wisdom from her life story. I was reading in the lobby during a main stage rehearsal for Paradigm Lost. Suddenly, it was break time and out poured all the comedians. As a college student, I was in awe.

Tina looked over and saw what I was reading and volunteered, "Wow, that's a great book. It's such a sad story what happened to Gilda." Honestly, I didn't really hear everything she said; I just thought it was cool that one of the actors was talking to me!

Then Kevin piped up from behind his cigarette, "If you want to succeed in improv, buddy, you need to give up reading autobiographies of comedians. Instead, read a breadth of history and current events. Be ready for any suggestion the audience throws at ya, 'cause you won't have time to ask someone on stage in the heat of the moment, 'What was *The War of the Roses*?' "

HOW TO REACT QUICKLY TO ANY SITUATION

> *"It opens you up that anything is viable as an idea. Sometimes in sitcoms you're handed stuff and you go, 'Well, this is illogical. No one would ever do this.' I think the atmosphere of Second City is everything happens, anything can happen, and you just have to justify it and find a way to get there. And, that's what a sitcom is: wild emotional swings for the sake of being funny." - Scott Adsit*[13]

It was said to aspiring comedians across the country during that time, "If you want to see the best improv actor who performs from the top of his intelligence, go to Chicago and watch Scott Adsit."

I had the rare opportunity night after night over the course of 18 months to watch Adsit in action. What made him so funny and quick-witted wasn't a storage of jokes, but instead that he read widely. Adsit was always devouring a newspaper, magazine, or novel. He worked hard at possessing a breadth of knowledge.

Breadth of knowledge is what enables comedians to react quickly to any situation and create fresh new material on an on-going basis. The more you know about current events, trends, and how they connect with history, the better you become at Trivial Pursuit and writing messages.

Leaders who excel lead from the overflow. Men and women who are devouring wisdom from prevailing practitioners are better equipped to adjust in fast-moving environments. On the flip side, leaders who lead out of memory and "that's just the way we've always done it" tend to dizzy themselves in circles while creating cul-de-sacs for the Kingdom. We have a name for this tribe of leaders: denominations.

READ WIDELY

Going back to the break time in the lobby, Kevin Dorff went on to explain to me from behind his cigarette: "Read history. Always be learning about areas you're not interested in so that you're ready for anything on stage. Grab the book *An Incomplete Education* and memorize it."

And that book is exactly what this poor college kid asked for as a gift at Christmas.

Too often in Christian leadership we become short-sighted and don't stretch ourselves. We just hang out with people who look like us and read stuff that validates our opinions. With the 21st Century's availability of lightning-fast information through tablets and smart phones, it's a shame that education is shunned in the face of fear of the unknown.

Remember this comedy secret because it translates directly toward prevailing leadership cultures: avoid information cocoons by reading widely and attending conferences. Refuse to only ingest what your denomination or online tribe spoon-feeds you. Stretch out the menu and try something from another food group.

Reading widely now equips you for bold leadership later. Because I am always reading, I am able to do our popular Live Q+A's at Life Church, call audibles with last minute changes, and respond to current events in messages.

As leaders, we must maintain a posture of learning outside our scope of ministry. When we read widely, we work from a vast pool of resources—we work from the top of our intelligence. When we read widely, we can make faster decisions on the spot. And when we read widely, we know what *The War of the Roses* was all about.

WRITING THE MESSAGE

When I sit down to think through an upcoming message, I want to write from the overflow of what God is already doing in me. If I'm regularly hungry for God's Word and I'm taking the time to be less on Facebook and more in The Book, messages will come more freely from within me.

Here's what I've learned in message prep: everything in your life can end up in a good sermon. As you read widely, you will uncover nuggets that will enhance your messages. As you journey through life, the discoveries you make and adventures you take can spice up any sermon.

I am always on the lookout for sermon material. If you have a bad memory, write things down that speak to you. If you don't write it down, you will probably lose it forever.

It's not uncommon when I'm watching the evening news for my wife to see me whip out my iPhone and write down a statistic that newscaster just mentioned. Having a collection of nuggets helps enhance future messages and impact people with God's Message. When I sit down with my big idea and key scripture, I will periodically roll out these nuggets I've collected to see if I can connect the dots. The more stories I can tell, the better.

The most successful comedians excel at taking the audience through a story. If you're preaching for life-change, reject giving lectures and instead tell stories. Here's why: executive decisions begin in the prefrontal cortex. This area of the brain activates chemicals and synapses more rapidly when the brain can *visualize* what it is hearing. Stories paint a picture for the brain to digest.

God wired our minds to remember pictures and stories. That's why movies are more popular than lectures. Jesus used parables to reveal Kingdom truths because He knew the average person can remember stories better than prepositional truths.

STRUCTURE FOR MAXIMUM STICKINESS

The average person who walks out of a church service completely forgets the entire message by the time they hit the parking lot. If you don't believe me, next Sunday run out to the departing car of a first-time guest and have them roll down their window to recite your main points.

You can either deny this truth, be deflated by this reality, or make a *Holy Shift* and do something about it. Here is how to structure your message for maximum stickiness:

- Have one big idea you're trying to get across. Not two. Not three. One. You can only make a Detroit Lions fan remember one thing from church that Sunday.

- Your one big idea has to be tweetable. If it's longer than 140 characters, it will not stick in people's brains. Social media has conditioned the human brain to think in sound bytes.

- Have three stories or ideas that reinforce the big idea. Stories trump lectures.

I promise you that if you make the *Holy Shift* and do these three things, even the unchurched, half-awake boyfriend who was dragged to church by his nagging girlfriend will remember your message.

FEED YOUR BRAIN (LITERALLY)

As I work on messages, I intentionally feed my brain. Neurologists will tell you that the human brain is a glucose hog. The more you concentrate on something, the more sugar is takes for your brain to focus.

If you're working in an office, have snacks and stay hydrated. If you're at Starbucks, treat yourself to some whipped cream on that coffee. Your brain is working overtime to connect the dots on your material and is burning through glucose at a high rate. Feed your brain (literally).

Studies have also shown that your mind can only concentrate for 18 minutes at a time.

Have you seen TED Talks online? What's the common denominator of these viral messages? They are all capped at 18 minutes in length. This is because that is how long an audience can concentrate at one time before they burn off too much glucose.

During message prep, take breaks every 18 minutes. Like Steve Jobs, I take breaks all the time and go for walks. It allows my brain to reset and refocus.

Additionally, the human brain can only work in a positive emotional climate. This isn't hyperbole; this is neuroscience. If you are trying to flesh out messages under stress, you are working against yourself.

On the biological level, the leader who writes messages at the last minute on Saturday night is fighting their own brain. Stress on the mind always releases cortisol into your system. Cortisol triggers fight or flight reactions, which does not always lead to clear thinking.

You are better off writing messages when you are relaxed and in a positive emotional climate. In this environment, the human brain releases positive chemicals that unleash your imagination. Again, this is neuroscience. As the leader, you control what kind of emotional climate you will be in.

Here's a message prep hack: if you are under a lot of stress with a deadline for a message, there's a simple way to change your emotional climate.

The human brain survives on three things: oxygen, glucose, and relationships. If you're stressed, go for a walk to increase oxygen intake. Grab a snack to up your glucose levels. And reach out to a friend to talk for ten minutes. Neuroscience proves that being connected with a friend drops stress hormones by 50%. I think this is why, in John 17, Jesus prays for His disciples to be connected together.

YOU GOTTA KNOW WHEN TO HOLD 'EM

Comedy and preaching are similar to a game of poker in that having a strong sense of timing can mean the difference between hitting the jackpot or slinking away from the table in shame.

Every time I share a story at live speaking engagements, I have to pace the story with proper timing of the unfolding events. If my timing is right, I get big laughs. If I'm off, it comes off as clunky and awkward.

Stories are king and timing is everything. Don't just give your audience the big idea; take them on a journey that builds toward a memorable payoff.

I highly recommend that you watch and study passionate communicators to learn better pacing and timing: TED Talks, churches that post video podcasts, and comedy specials are great sources. All of these free online resources will help you develop a better sense of timing.

THREE IS A MAGIC NUMBER

She was pretty. She was shapely. She was a man.

Leaders speak a lot. When writing your next message, remember to write and speak in three's. If you are going to share any kind of list in your message, threes set up a comic payoff.

There are three little pigs, three stooges, and three rules for owning a mogwai named Gizmo. (The movie *Gremlins*, anyone? Children of the 80s unite!)

For some reason, the human brain laughs in threes. The first two items in the triplet set the pattern and the third item breaks the pattern. Breaking the pattern heightens the tension and creates the surprise, usually resulting in laughter.

Here's another example of threes in action from everyone's favorite motivational speaker, Matt Foley: "First off, I am 35 years old. I am divorced. And I live in a van down by the river!"

When you're speaking or writing, do it in threes. It's just plain funnier.

CALLBACKS

Callbacks are a clever use of timing for leaders who speak or write. They do three things:

1. Callbacks add an exclamation mark to the point you are making.

2. Callbacks give a wink and a nod to the audience following along (which makes you look smarter than you are and builds trust with your audience).

3. Callbacks signal to the audience that you are concluding your thought and moving on to another.

In improv there's a saying: "The end is in the beginning." When you're speaking in front of a crowd and you've made them laugh, move on to something fresh and new. Later, when no one's expecting it, make a quick reference to what made them laugh earlier. That's how a callback works.

Perhaps the greatest example of callbacks in the history of modern comedy happened during the 1992 *Academy Awards*. Jack Palance won the Oscar for Best Supporting Actor at the age of 73 for the movie *City Slickers*. To prove his agility as an actor, Palance performed three one-handed push-ups to a delighted live television audience of millions.

Billy Crystal turned this moment into an impromptu gag: "I told Jack just before the ceremony, 'Decaf, Jack, decaf!' "

To the delight of the audience, the callbacks continued throughout the night, with Crystal announcing that Palance:

"... was backstage on the Stairmaster."

"... just bungee-jumped off the Hollywood sign."

"... rendezvoused with the space shuttle in orbit."

"... fathered all the children in that last production number."

"... has been named People Magazine's Sexiest Man Alive!"

At the end of the broadcast, Crystal told the audience he would like to see them again, "But I've just been informed Jack Palance will be hosting next year." The audience erupted in laughter and Billy Crystal cemented his status as a beloved host of the Oscars.

Callbacks can create a solid thread through a message that unites and endears. This makes this simple use of timing an especially strong specialty tool in the communicator's arsenal. It can punch up your communications as a leader and should be leveraged whenever possible.

THE SECRET TO COMEDY IS TIMING

Timing is also paramount in our overly-saturated 24/7 social media landscape. Our smart phones have become the 21st Century version of a smoke break. We carry our digital leashes everywhere, addicted to status updates and instant communication. Because information is always flowing, we can become numb to the power and influence of social media.

In short, too many churches do Facebook badly. Very often a well-meaning Sunday School teacher will post a Bible verse on a Saturday night expecting it to go viral, only to face disappointment and discouragement when five days later they receive a grand total of one Facebook Like.

Timing is everything when it comes to leveraging the free power of social media. If you want to engage your people with Instagram and Twitter (and you should—it's free!), remember that timing is everything.

Posting online is about strategic interruptions. If your message is important, you need to be mindful of what time you are posting.

At Life Church, we have discovered that posting to our Twitter and Facebook feeds at 7am (before they go to work), 12pm (during their lunch break), and 7pm (when people are checking their smart phones while simultaneously catching up on their DVR or Netflix) are the best times to reach our people and achieve some level of contagious enthusiasm.

We have also discovered the power of tagging photos. Facebook has a free feature that allows you to identify Facebook users in your photos. We have a photographer take random photos during the Sunday services and post them on our Facebook Page every Monday night. Then we take extra time to individually tag people in the photos and include our website in the comments section of each photo. This causes these photos to pop up on the Facebook feeds of tagged people's friends throughout the region, increasing our church's visibility for free while also giving our church instant credibility: "Hey, I didn't know Olivia served kids at a church! That's so cool!"

Churches can create a hunger for their posts by not posting frequently. I know that sounds counter-intuitive, but it is how actors are trained to market themselves.

Take Brad Pitt for example. You will go months and months without hearing about him or seeing stories about him online. When he's two weeks out from headlining a new movie release, you suddenly see his face smiling back at you everywhere and stories about his personal life pop up online. Is that random coincidence? Nope, it is strategic interruption.

The thing is, church leaders live, eat, and breathe church world. We are passionate about reaching people far from God and so we are constantly thinking and praying about what could be and what should be. Never apologize for wanting to fulfill the Great Commission, just remember that your congregation isn't always as consumed by the Call as you are.

Regular people live, eat, and breathe about ordinary things, school, work, finances, politics, etc. And that's okay. Give yourself permission to go dark during quieter seasons. Resurface strategically when regular people are more spiritually attuned (January, Easter, September, and Christmas). You will get more power for your punch when you are in rhythm with natural seasons of momentum.

For example, we share vision and stories of life transformation via social media throughout the month of January. This matches where regular people are focused in the New Year. In February, our Facebook and Twitter feeds strategically focus more on Scriptures and the character of God. This cools the jets and allows our people to breathe in the gospel.

I believe God uses these quieter seasons to create a holy hunger that builds and builds until crescendoing at Easter, when we rev back up with massive outreach endeavors.

Timing is important whether you're a church leader or Brad Pitt's agent.

The quiet periods where you hear nothing about Brad Pitt create a subtle but real hunger within his fans. When it's time to fire up the marketing machine and get people in the seats, Brad Pitt's team strategically gets his face on the cover of *People Magazine*, buys advertising for the upcoming film, and covertly releases juicy insider stories for gossip columns.

Timing is everything and the same principle can be applied to churches trying to engage people who don't always enjoy going to church!

DON'T BE TIRED

Part of leveraging timing in comedy and leadership is making sure you're performing at the top of your game. If you're feeling run down, it will reflect in how you present yourself.

Two things happen when you're tired: you have depressed cognitive ability and you're sluggish. This leads to shoddy work and/or shoddy attitudes, and that doesn't lift up your team. Being tired just drags everyone else down.

Don't walk around telling everyone you're tired. Nobody cares if you're tired. If you're a comedian, the show must go on. If you're leading a church, Sunday is always just days away. Don't be tired.

Do whatever you have to do to not be tired. Exercise regularly. Seek creative inspiration. Drink a Red Bull and get your wings. Turn off the TV and go to bed earlier. Just don't tell everyone you're tired.

Also, don't be drunk. This probably goes without saying, but you'd be surprised. For instance, I have an awesome volunteer in our church named Ben. Early on in launching our church, I gave Ben the assignment to create a silhouette of the word "LIFE" using plywood and canned stage lighting.

At 10:30 the night before our church's first public worship service, Ben called. Here's what I heard through his excitedly slurred speech: "Uh, Jon? I cut out the letters! They're nine feet tall each!"

He texted me photos of his creation and, to make a long story short, he did the exact opposite of the task I had given him. We had gargantuan, Wheel of Fortune style physical letters to haul onto our stage. Turns out Ben was drunk while doing ministry.

The moral of this story? Don't be drunk. And definitely don't be tired.

CREATIVITY CONSTIPATION

Cranking out fresh material is hard work. Every comedian and leader shares the same struggle of dry seasons when the creative juices are quenched and decisions become tougher to make.

I remember talking with comedy director Mick Napier about what to do when you don't know what to do. He gave me a piece of advice that rings true for comedians and leaders: "Start with anything and let your brain catch up."

When you're stuck in a rut, there is only one way out of the cul-de-sac of mediocrity; make a bold choice and move forward with the ensemble. Don't worry about the details; you'll figure them out along the way. Make a statement and go for it.

This applies to teams too. People will follow the person who is most decisive and paints the best picture of the future. That person needs to be you. There are three directions you can lead people:

1. You may choose leading backward, preserving what made you succeed in the first place. This type of leading works well for museum curators and monument builders.

    Leading backwards is safe because it's familiar, predictable, and unchanging. This feels safe because it is risk-free. But following Christ means being free to risk.

2. You may choose leading sideways. You don't really move forward or backward when you're going sideways . . . instead you just maintain things. When a leader is unclear or indecisive, paralysis dictates immobilization.

    Sideways leading works well for politicians and 30-year-old men living in their momma's basement playing World of Warcraft at 3 a.m. They are the wind testers, the status quo, and the settled.

3. I'm urging you to courageously choose leading forward. These are the risk-taking mavericks who move ahead into the unknown. Forward leading can be lonely at each new initiative; by nature you are in front of everyone else. But that's precisely where vision and faith collide!

    Most people dream, but a dream without faith is a fantasy. God-infused dreams fueled by faith become reality, but only if you're leading forward.

The best comedy and leadership decisions started somewhere, so pick a where and go explore. You can't just wander through life as a gun collector, storing up treasures in a glass walnut case. At some point, you have to shoot those guns!

FINAL SERMON POINTERS

After I have my message on paper, I memorize it. You never see a good comic go on-stage and read from a notebook into a microphone. It just doesn't look professional.

My goal is to remove any barrier between someone far from God and the gospel. Truth be told, standing behind a podium creates a physical barrier. Make a *Holy Shift* to do the hard work and own the message.

If I can memorize my message, it impacts people to a greater degree and causes my audience to be thinking: "Wow, he's preaching without notes? He must really mean what he's saying!"

The good news is that if you structured your message for maximum stickiness, then it should be easy to remember your tweetable big idea and the three stories that support it. When I'm running through my message in preparation, I visualize a key object or person in the next story I want to tell. This keeps my mind sharp and in the moment with my audience. Stories are much easier to remember than doctrinal points.

I highly recommend practicing your message over and over throughout the week. If you have a long commute, turn off talk radio and run through your message silently in your mind.

The more you connect the dots between stories in your mind, the greater clarity you will have Sunday morning. Rehearsing a message in your mind creates stronger neural pathways for later recollection. Everybody wins when you practice your message multiple times.

When I come to the big idea that I need my audience to remember, I set up the point by saying, "Hey, listen up and tweet these next words." This resets the audience's minds and makes them think, "Whoah, I better focus so I can share this on Facebook!" My video worker takes that cue and fires a slide with the statement I want to communicate, I point people to the screen to focus them, and then I just read what's on the screen. That's how you get your key point communicated without losing your mind! Remember stories and leverage technology with key points.

If my words are 40% of what I communicate on Sunday morning, my body language and attitude account for 60% of what the audience remembers. I attack every Sunday morning like a bull in a china shop. Just as you don't want to go see a lethargic, unsure comedian sweat it out on stage, I don't want to see a boring preacher reinforce my church stereotypes on a Sunday morning. The reason most people don't go to church is because they have already been to one.

Abraham Lincoln once said, "When I hear a man preach, I like to see him act as if he was fighting bees." Me too!

The key is to take the memorized message and pepper it with strong, confident body language and Spirit-fueled passion. If I really believe in what I'm saying, I'm going to preach it with conviction: shoulders squared, gut sucked in, energy pouring out of my mouth!

John Wesley's approach to preaching was awesome. "I set myself on fire and people come to watch me burn." That's my aim every single Sunday morning at Life Church!

The Prince of Preachers, C.H. Spurgeon, sums up passionate preaching best:

> *"If you desire to see souls converted; if you would place crowns upon the head of the Savior and lift His throne high, then be*

filled with zeal. For, under God, the way of the world's conversion must be by the zeal of the church . . .

"Zeal is stimulated by the thought of the eternal future. It looks with tearful eyes down to the flames of hell, and it cannot sleep. It looks up with longing for the glories of heaven, and it cannot but rouse itself.

"It feels that time is short compared with the work to be done; therefore, it devotes all that it has to the cause of its Lord."

9

LESS CATHEDRAL, MORE COMEDY CLUB

"Everyone said to Vincent van Gogh, 'You can't be a great painter, you only have one ear.'

"And you know what he said? 'I can't hear you.'" - Steve Carell

Before someone can become theologically-aware, they first must feel environmentally-secure. Because of stereotypes and bad experiences, the average person does not feel comfortable walking into a new church for the first time.

Anxiety and fear will cloud their experience if you do not address the elephant in the room. It's because of this that I believe we should aim for Sundays to feel like less cathedral and more comedy club.

UNDER-PROMISE AND OVER-DELIVER

"The best thing about improv is that no matter how bad your show is, it's only 30 minutes, and never exists again. The worst thing is no matter how good your show is, it's only 30 minutes, and never exists again." - Mick Napier[14]

Comedians have the luxury of reinvention because people love to laugh and will seek out comedy. Churches do not have this luxury because lost people are looking for a reason to mentally check out and never return to your church. If you blow it on Sunday with a person far from God, they will quickly become far from your church.

In today's world, it is still culturally-assumed that if you have questions about faith, your best bet is to walk into a church on a Sunday morning. The culture assumes Sunday is going to meet their needs. Because of this, leaders need to focus and leverage the bulk of their planning, budget, and talent toward preparing for the Sunday morning worship experience.

In short, if you want to reach lost people, your church needs to reduce the clutter of mid-week programming and echo the Monster Truck commercials: "Sunday, Sunday, Sunday!"

Pointing people toward the Sunday morning worship experience is key. Our culture finds that golden hour acceptable for seeking God. Tons of tools are at your disposal for engaging lost people: Twitter, Facebook, direct mail, etc. You can read up on best practices elsewhere (I recommend Michael Hyatt's bestselling book, *Platform*). I want to turn our attention toward the hype behind creating a crowd.

Hype that lives up to the hype is GREAT. Delivering on your amplified promises can build a reputation and momentum. However, when you promise something great yet deliver a sub-par product, you stain your credibility and empty seats. And let's be honest, this happens a LOT in leadership circles and within church world.

Advertising a bad product just means even more people are aware that your product stinks. We want to think like a comedy club by under-promising and over-delivering.

In a classic 1995 Second City scene featuring comedians Adam McKay (*SNL*) and Scott Adsit (*30 Rock*), the premise is under-promised: a mundane job review. No hype. No huge promises about what the audience is to expect. Just a simple under-promise of a routine, run-of-the-mill job review.

Because the audience isn't expecting to have their minds blown, the elements of surprise, discovery, and delight are in motion. Adsit provides a memorable turn as a dim-witted CEO with a 51 I.Q. who tells his low-level HR director, "I could crush you like a cloud."

As the scene progresses, you continue to see two skilled improvisers transform the run-of-the-mill into the extraordinary. In short, they over-deliver. That's where the comedy is coming from.

The surprise engages people's minds and takes them to a new place. The laughter and applause is an acknowledgment that the improvisers wisely under-promised and over-delivered, which generates buzz and interest, resulting in more people eventually experiencing the product.

People already assume from past experiences that the church is home to mediocrity. They've experienced the sermons that put them into a coma and awkwardly sat through Great Aunt Ginny warbling her off-key vocal chords through horrible solos that are tragically called "Specials" and are anything but. Over-promising an activity or event that is executed poorly leads to reinforcing these stereotypes.

If you're going to jump on Twitter on Saturday night and promise that this coming Sunday will be the best Sunday ever, you'd better deliver big time. And there is a time and a place for those tweets. Just remember, leaders shape expectations. Every leader either creates expectations or allows expectations to take shape.

You can also create a culture of surprise and delight by consistently hitting home runs. Your reputation for quality will organically birth quantity.

Remember these equations:

> Over-promise + Under-deliver =
> Reputation Stainer + Momentum Killer
>
> Under-promise + Over-deliver =
> Spontaneous Buzz + Authentic Growth

THE BIG REVEAL

"Nobody expects the Spanish Inquisition! Our chief weapon is surprise..." - Monty Python

Let me tackle this *Holy Shift* principle from another angle. Martin de Maat gave us a great exercise in one of our comedy courses. He gave us each a secret before we started improvising our scene. We weren't supposed to talk about it; each person's secret was to be their motivation.

The exercise was incredible as great comedy erupted in those improvised scenes. At the end, we found out the big reveal. Martin had told each of us the same thing, "It's your partner's birthday."

The secret motivation was the under-promise because it was not shared. The action and dialogue was heightened because each person was acting like it was the other's birthday... without actually saying, "Hey, Happy Birthday!" This made every word and action an over-delivery of pure joy.

In leadership, you have a hand in shaping the future. If you keep expectations low and raise the bar for execution high, you shape a future of surprise and delight. When looking at your next big event or message series, layer your plans with this *Holy Shift*. Under-promise what is to come and then work your tail off to over-deliver the results.

As comedy director Del Close once observed, "A scene is almost never about what the players think it's going to be about!" When you under-promise an endeavor as a leader, you actually free yourself to enjoy the journey. If the expectations are low, the freedom is available to explore and fly higher.

VIRAL SKETCHES DON'T EQUAL MOVIE SUCCESS

MacGruber. Ugh. Another *SNL* sketch-turned-movie. Another box office BOMB. Seriously, who thought *MacGruber* on the big screen was a great idea? It joins *Ladies Man*, *A Night at the Roxbury*, and *It's Pat* as great viral *SNL* sketches but horrible Hollywood pitches.

The premises behind these sketches are great on the micro level but not successfully duplicated on the macro level. How often do we take something that works in a specific micro context and try to franchise its success in another venue?

The institutional church can learn from *Saturday Night Live* on this: viral sketches don't equal movie success. Sure, there's the rare *Blues Brothers/Wayne's World* success (or in church world, Elevation Church/North Point Church). But those are acts of God that aren't necessarily meant to be duplicated and replicated nationwide.

Think about it. Where in the Bible does God perform the exact same miracle twice? The Scriptures don't share stories of duplication or imitation but instead stories of men and women who boldly follow revelation.

If you are a church leader, please lean in closely and please allow these words to sink in: you are not the next Andy Stanley or Tim Keller. And that's by God's design. Learn from them? Yes. Replicate them? No. Instead of replicating the culture of cathedrals (which are largely empty), let's seek the creative aesthetics of comedy clubs (which are largely full).

God doesn't want or need you to copy what everyone else is already doing or to fill someone else's shoes; He wants you to fill yours! Just because something "works" in one place doesn't mean it will succeed in another. Marching around a city worked once for Jericho, but it is not meant to be a prescription for God's intervention. When we try to duplicate the miraculous, we erase the very circumstances that make it miraculous.

Continue reading and learning from other leaders who are seeing God move. Ask deep, probing questions. But like any good fisherman, eat the meat and spit out the bones. Church world is not one-size-fits-all. Listen to God and lead forward.

Leaders, reject the temptation to act older/larger than you really are. Be content with your current age. Church planters, beware the trap of leading/operating systems that don't fit your current size. Don't plant the church in your head; plant the church grounded in reality.

Act your age. It makes the journey forward simpler and more honest.

BEWARE KING TUT'S FOSSILS

Think back with me to 1975 to Steve Martin's infamous *King Tut* sketch and *Saturday Night Live*'s Not-Ready-for-Prime-Time-Players. Viewers were buzzing about the dancing Egyptians and silly lyrics playing out on their TV screens.

SNL made history from its beginning with risk-taking ideas in their programming. *SNL* loves to replay old sketches on anniversary specials over and over again, reliving the glory days. Good material, yes; however, your past doesn't promise the present. Beware King Tut's fossils.

Back in the day, Belushi and Aykroyd were golden in the ratings. There was nothing on TV like *SNL*. Over time, the formula grew predictable and ratings dropped. Critics habitually labeled NBC's institution as Saturday Night DEAD.

Just because your program worked in the past doesn't guarantee it will work thirty-five years later. Let's lead churches that are living in the present, not the past. The past may seem comfortable due to its predictability, but it reeks of rust.

Culture changes. The task of engaging an ever-changing culture is to try new programming. Take risks. Replicating someone is inauthentic. Don't rest on the laurels and fossils of the past. Do whatever it takes.

THE DIFFERENCE BETWEEN DISNEY AND PIXAR

Let me frame this another way. We all grew up on Disney movies, right? I bet if I were to ask you to list ten of your favorite animated films from childhood, almost all of them would be Disney films.

This probably won't be the case for children growing up in today's world. When my oldest son was a toddler, he didn't have Mickey Mouse wallpaper in his bedroom. Instead it's covered with *Cars* and *Toy Story*. My daughter is growing up in an age where young women are encouraged to be *Brave* and to *Let It Go*. This is because the freshness of Pixar eclipsed Disney's tired old formulas to create a new legacy.

The tipping point for Pixar was in the early 1990's. At the time, *The Little Mermaid* was THE standard in motion picture animation. That's when the little known production start-up pitched Tom Hanks. Hanks' response: "You don't want me to sing, do you?"

Pixar assured him that *Toy Story* would be different. They quietly wrote out their own secret rules of story-telling:

- No songs
- No "I want" moment
- No happy village
- No love story
- No villain

As *Toy Story* went into production, Disney bosses freaked out. Disney contacted a well-known, established songwriter for his take. Without knowing about Pixar's secret rules, he said *Toy Story* needed:

- Songs
- An "I want" moment
- A happy village
- A love story
- A villain

Pixar broke all the rules. And in the process, they built a better story.

That's what I'm begging you to do. Don't try living out somebody else's story. God didn't tell you to write their story; He wants you to live out yours!

10

HOW TO HANDLE THE CRITICS

"Generally, I've found that a heckler in an improv audience is just enjoying the show so much that they want to be in it."
- Scott Adsit

After Jesus' resurrection, the Bible records a curious moment. Basically, Peter is hanging out with Jesus when another disciple, John, catches Peter's eye:

"When Peter saw him, he said to Jesus, "Lord, what about this man?" Jesus said to him, 'If it is my will that he remain until I come, what is that to you? You follow me!'" - John 21:21-22 (ESV)

I love this passage because it sums up one of the biggest struggles facing leaders today: compulsively comparing. Whether it's curiosity or insecurity or envy, we all tend to pull a Peter.

Mistake #1 is taking our eyes off Jesus and focusing on someone else in ministry. Any time our gaze gets fixated on anything other than Jesus, things get out of whack in our lives! Don't pull a Peter; keep your focus on Jesus!

Mistake #2 is when we compare ourselves to another leader. We hop on Google or read a gossip site masquerading as "Christian news" and lament. "Lord, what about Matt Chandler/Perry Noble/Francis Chan over there?" We aspire for someone else's platform and notoriety. We want what they have. The problem is that God has not called you to write their story; He's called you to live out yours. This isn't junior high gym class; the comparisons need to stop!

The darker side of leadership envy is when we look down our noses in judgment toward a fellow Christian leader. "Lord, what about that church? What about that guy? I've heard about them . . ." Because we are not rooted in Christ, we try to uproot someone else to make ourselves feel warm and fuzzy. But that's not a warm fuzzy you're feeling in your heart—it's sin.

There's no need to either wish you were your favorite rock star pastor or to appoint yourself the captain of the church police squad. Either way, Jesus has the same response: "What is that to you? You follow me!"

In other words, Jesus is saying that you have not been called to reach people in John's unique way. Your concern is not what John is doing; your concern needs to be what Jesus is doing!

I'm going to plant my feet here just a bit longer to double-down on the idea behind John 21. I firmly believe that there would be greater Kingdom impact and healthier Christian leaders in every town across the country if all the pastors would stop pulling Peters and start pulling for each other. Territorialism among church leaders is not biblical.

When we're fretting over other churches (that we are not responsible for, by the way), what's really happening is that our insecurities are being exposed to the open air. Insecure leaders don't shape the world. The solution is to stop looking to others for approval, root yourself securely in Christ (Colossians 2:7) and "root" for the other churches in town.

If you struggle with insecurity, please go read Matthew 3:16-17. When Jesus came up out of the baptismal waters of the Jordan, God the Father declared publicly and unmistakably that He was completely pleased with the Son. If you have Christ living inside of you and He is your identity, than those words are true for you too. God is already completely pleased with you because of Christ.

If you are securely favored by God in Christ, you have nothing to feel insecure about. You don't have to compare yourself to other leaders because you are already completely accepted by the Father.

Further, I've always found this account from the life of John the Baptist striking:

> *"The next day again John was standing with two of his disciples, and he looked at Jesus as he walked by and said, 'Behold, the Lamb of God!' The two disciples heard him say this, and they followed Jesus."* - John 1:35-37 (ESV)

Don't miss this. John celebrates another ministry! When John's disciples hop over to Jesus' church, John the Baptist does not become insecure, territorial, or freak out . . . he blesses Jesus' ministry, speaks highly of Jesus' ministry, and encourages others to join in what God is doing through Jesus.

How refreshing would it be if we all shared John's attitude in our towns and cities? Let's reject carnality and instead celebrate and encourage what God is doing in and through other ministries. After all, it takes all different flavors of churches to reach all different flavors of people.

In our region of Michigan, we have a rainbow of fruit flavors to choose from on Sunday mornings: denominational churches, independent churches, quiet and introspective churches, loud and modern churches. We are all worshiping the same God and Savior. I think that's why Paul wrote:

> *"When one of you says, 'I am a follower of Paul,' and another says, 'I follow Apollos,' aren't you acting just like people of the world? The one who plants and the one who waters work together with the same purpose. And both will be rewarded for their own hard work." - 1 Corinthians 3:3, 8*

When we launched Life Church in Saginaw, Michigan, I worked very hard to communicate over and over that we were not starting a new church to compete with other ministries; our heart is to complete the Body. John 21 frees us to be who God is shaping us to be. "What is that to you?"

NOBODY KNOWS YOU EXIST

"Declare what you honestly want and live that vision fearlessly."
- Mick Napier

Once you're ready to engage people far from God in new ways, you need to pound the drums and get their attention. Whether you're an up-and-coming comic or a leader with a message, attention spans are extremely finite. Audiences get information from multiple sources, making it fractured and distracted. You must be willing to deliver your message in multiple ways.

For example, NBC used to be king in late night entertainment. After Johnny Carson's retirement, everything began to rapidly fragment. While Jay Leno tried to hold the traditional mantle, post-Johnny comedy giants like Conan O'Brien have seen the power of harnessing social media.

Amplifying your presence in an increasingly cluttered media landscape is key. He who leverages YouTube reaches a new generation. For example, Jay Leno's Twitter account boasted merely 376,000 followers while Conan O'Brien's Twitter reaches over five million.

Leno represents the pre-Johnny era where stars were stars and didn't fraternize with mere humans. Hollywood actors protected their image and were rarely heard from until they had a movie or product to promote on *The Tonight Show*. Conan, on the other hand, is paving the way in this post-Johnny era. Twitter/blogs/Facebook are leveraged as social tools that spotlight your presence 24/7. Jimmy Fallon *Yes, Anded* both of them by leveraging social media hashtags as part of *The Tonight Show* broadcasts.

In 1993, the obsession in television was don't give anything away. Keep everything buttoned-down until the moment you go live. Twenty years later, we live in a world where there are no surprises, everything goes everywhere, and there is incredible awareness. Amidst all the media clutter, nobody knows you exist. For the sake of your church's mission, you have to do something about that.

MYSTERIOUS GHOST CHURCHES

"This is not the way that I watch television, but I had to make a choice, and I think this is the way." - Conan O'Brien, on the rise of Twitter

While pursuing my undergrad in theater, one of the final required courses was Marketing Yourself 101. Seriously, we studied and practiced how to stand out in a crowded field overflowing with wannabe actors and professionals. The days of sending out cold-call headshots and waiting for a job offer ended years ago.

One of the tips we were taught by folks in the entertainment industry was to get your name into agents' heads every single week. People are busy and building up chips through strategic interruption and ongoing relationships help keep your face and name on their radar.

This is absolutely true for churches. Too many leaders get frustrated because their people "forget" about upcoming events or ooze less passion than the leader. Um, maybe its because they have a life beyond your church. Remembering that nobody knows you exist will help motivate and create multiple communication touches. Remember, vision is about communicating the same compelling idea thousands of times in millions of ways.

Church plants specifically have to grapple with this principle. When you're portable, you are like a mysterious ghost church that magically appears for a few brief hours early on a Sunday morning only to melt away by 1 p.m. The rest of the week, your church plant doesn't exist except as an idea or concept. Nobody knows you exist, so getting your name and vision out there consistently and broadly is key to, well, survival.

THE BETTY WHITE PHENOMENON

Walt Disney never met a technology he was afraid of. Disney constantly adapted: animation to talkies to motion pictures to theme parks to television. He always embraced new things. People who worked around Disney said his mantra was to adapt or die.

Church leaders must be constant students of the rapidly evolving technology at the dawn of this Digital Age. Twenty years ago the church world experts told us to start a newsletter. Five years ago we were told to start a blog. Today we're told to get on Twitter, Instagram, and Origamzani. Ok, I made that last name up just to make sure you were still tracking with me (although I think Origamzani is a million dollar idea if you want to start it, just thank me later). Nobody knows you exist until you intentionally penetrate their world with the Gospel like a missionary.

As you engage your message with others, connections and relationships will materialize. This is what made Betty White famous again. White's recent reemergence as a beloved comedienne began with Lifetime Channel airing old reruns of *The Golden Girls*. Ratings spiked as college girls were introduced to the shenanigans of no-nonsense Dorothy, witless Rose, man-starved Blanche, and wise-cracking Sophia. Betty White was suddenly cool again.

The Snickers candy bar company took that momentum and had the brilliant idea to film a commercial starring Betty White that aired during the 2010 Super Bowl. People loved the message and grew fond of the aging comedienne.

The combination of college kids, Snickers, and the 2010 Super Bowl led to a Facebook campaign. At the grassroots level, people took their affection and fondness for Betty White and channeled it toward petitioning *Saturday Night Live* to invite White to host the show.

It worked. In May of 2010, Betty White became the oldest guest host on the live comedy program. The result? Betty White hosting *SNL* scored huge ratings. The message had come full circle: from retirement obscurity to ratings superstar.

Of course the "Get Betty on *SNL*" campaign worked. It appealed to the digital generation's culture. Your church can tap into this same phenomenon as part of its mission. The message of the church isn't compromised, but like all missionaries, the method flexibly adapts.

AMPLIFY, AMPLIFY, AMPLIFY YOUR MESSAGE

I often hear from well-meaning leaders who want to see their churches grow yet fear it will somehow result in other Christians and churches in town feeling somehow inadequate or inferior. Listen, you are not responsible for how other Christians react. Never apologize for trying to fulfill the Great Commission!

If people really are destined for Hell unless Somebody saves them, and you have been called to lead the rescue in your town, amplify your message. Declare your intentions and fearlessly get the Word out.

If this results in negative comments from other churches in town, who cares? Everybody needs a hobby; your critics' hobby is just sitting back and watching you win!

Social media gives you the opportunity to either tear down people or influence others for Christ. Be a leader who lifts people up!

I thank God for the Internet. Online tools such as blogs and Twitter can help you rapidly engage with people far from God. Because of the technology, today's leaders can go further, faster.

Leveraging Facebook and other social media tools is not becoming "too worldly" or making it more about you and less about Jesus. I love how Donald Miller puts it:

> "Self promotion is not unholy. Occasionally I'll encounter some well-meaning religious person who thinks self promotion works against the fame of God. I whole-heartedly disagree. In his day, Billy Graham spent millions promoting himself and his crusades, all so people could come HEAR HIM TALK ABOUT GOD.
>
> "Those who know Mr. Graham would never see him as arrogant. He was over himself. But that didn't mean God didn't give him a personality and a mouth and later a microphone. Flowers bloom and mountains tower not to take attention from God, but to display His glory."[15]

The Christians in your town who complain about church advertisements and marketing are the exact same Christians who go to a church with a church sign out front. Um, that crusty old sign is an advertisement!

What's more, many church signs have the pastor's name listed on the bottom. If that's not self-promotion, I don't know what is!

In short, don't worry about what the Christian subculture in your area will think about your efforts to engage people far from God. No matter what you do, you will be misunderstood by either fellow Christians or lost people. I'd rather be misunderstood by fellow Christians in an attempt to make heaven crowded.

This isn't just me being flippant, it's entirely biblical. Take a look at John 6:66. Yes, the Scripture reference is 666, so I think you know where I'm headed with this example!

Earlier in chapter 6 of the Book of John, the crowds say to Jesus that they want a sign: "Do you have a Son of Man business card we can share with our unbelieving friends or a website we can point them to?"

Jesus responds to the crowds by sharing His true identity, which isn't what the religious people were expecting. And so in verse 66 the Bible says, "From this time many of His disciples turned away and no longer followed Him."

Wow, did you catch that? *Jesus had religious people walking out of His church!* Jesus was declaring the gospel clearly, but His method was being misunderstood. If religious people were even walking away from Jesus Christ's message, then don't be surprised when religious folk walk out of your church. Think about it; you're in good company if that happens!

At the end of the day, people are going to walk out of your church no matter what you do. As the leader, you cannot keep everyone happy. Your job is to define which people you're okay with leaving your church. Will it be the religious people who will just hop into another church down the street that feels more comfortable to them, or the people far from God who will go home and delete pursuing Christ from their life?

Personally, I want to reach people far from God with new life in Christ, so I'm going to do whatever it takes to enter their world with the gospel. This is exactly what Jesus and Paul and every other successful missionary in church history has done.

If my methods of sharing God's Message ticks off some misunderstanding people who are already Christ-followers, that's fine. There are lots of empty pews down the street for them to choose from. In the meantime, I'm rolling up my sleeves, cranking up my prayers, and doing whatever it takes to reach people far from God!

ONE CAUTION IN AMPLIFYING YOUR MESSAGE

Nobody knows you exist, so you want to leverage whatever tools you have in your tool belt. For me, that includes sharing my story about partying with Chris Farley two nights before he died and how God used that event to change the trajectory of my life toward pointing people to Jesus Christ. 99% of the time that story is successful in its intent. But there was one time when it almost backfired.

The weekend we held our very first preview worship service for Life Church, I was invited to be interviewed on our local NBC affiliate's morning news show. The live segments were to air beginning at 5:30am, which meant I was awake and in-studio at an ungodly hour. There was no preparation before the interview, meaning I was meeting the news anchor during the commercial break while getting situated under the hot studio lights at a time when I am normally unconscious in dreamy-dream land.

As the show came back from commercial break, the studio cameras went live and the anchor introduced the segment as a sit-down with a "man of the cloth" who years ago had partied with Chris Farley.

Everything was good and fine as I shared the story that opens this book on live morning television. That is, until the interviewer, who is a good guy and all, locked onto the sensational side of my story for what seemed like an eternity on live television. With hot studio lights and large booming cameras bearing down on me, I heard him press this question pointedly: "Were you partying with him?"

Have you ever had an out-of-body experience while you were in front of a group of people doing something important like giving a speech or something? Your mouth is talking somewhat intelligibly on the outside but inside you there's a dialogue flashing through your mind that is actively critiquing your experience in real-time? That's the experience that began happening to me while on the NBC television set. In fact, you can watch the video for yourself on our website, LifeChurchMichigan.com. The clip is funnier when you know what my internal dialogue was at the time.

As I was fumbling out an answer to his question on the outside, my internal mind envisioned a tiny little squirrel quietly waking up, yawning, and stretching its tiny little squirrel arms, and from the comfort of its cute little IKEA-inspired squirrel bed, innocently switching on its television to innocently start its happy day with my story about partying with Chris Farley.

I got through answering the question and discreetly held my breath as the reporter leaned in and tossed out his follow-up question: "Was he doing drugs at that time?"

The happy little squirrel inside my head was suddenly jolted out of his IKEA bed by a Drudge Report wailing news alert status that warned in ALL CAPS that something big and scary was on the horizon. The Keebler Elves, who happened to live in the same tree as our happy little squirrel, began putting down their workshop tools and peering into the windows trying to catch a glimpse of the television interview in the squirrel's bedroom.

My groggy mind tried to clumsily redirect the storyline back toward God and rich spiritual truths, but who am I kidding, I was melting on live television. That's when the reporter went all-in and TMZ'd me on live television with a question clawing for something sensational. "What kind of drugs?"

The happy little squirrel spontaneously exploded in a grisly scene of carnage and mayhem. Keebler Elves were crying hysterically and production on all Keebler Cookies had to be halted due to my interview going off-message that was destined for YouTube viral infamy.

Somewhere in the distance, I thought I could hear my Mom watching this at home and quietly crying.

In the interviewer's defense, he was just doing his job. He's a great guy with a big heart and a stellar reputation, but he didn't have a scripted mandate to help promote our church on his morning show. His goal was to keep the audience at home interested and, let's face it, the salacious personal details of celebrity lives grabs people's attention.

At the end of the day, I was thankful that I had the opportunity to share my story, invite people to church to hear God's Story, and that no actual squirrels or Keebler Elves were physically harmed during the television interview. That I'm aware of.

Nobody knows you exist, so don't be afraid to put yourself out there and amplify your message. Just make sure that you drink plenty of coffee and that you're healthy enough to laugh at yourself later if things get a little crazy and end up on YouTube.

HANDLING HECKLERS

"I love Disney World. It reminds me of my childhood. I mean before my two-year stint at Children's." - Debbie Downer

Rachel Dratch was brilliant as Debbie Downer on *Saturday Night Live*. Always ruining conversations and moments with her downers, Debbie Downer rocks.

Real-life Debbie Downers, however, do not rock. They are the exact opposite of rock. They are paper.

Real-life Debbie Downers are small-minded people in the audience who want to critically tear down the person on stage, ruining the experience for everyone. They are not for you, do not have a heart for your success, and they are acting out of selfishness.

Debbie's cousin, Chatty Cathy, is just as nasty. Chatty Cathy likes to make herself look bigger by gossiping about you. How do I define gossip? Any complaint passed to someone not in a position to fix the problem. Gossips will talk about you without talking to you.

Comedians know both Debbie Downer and Chatty Cathy all by a single word: hecklers.

First, a word to you if you're a heckler.

Does your lead pastor have a white-hot, God-ordained vision for where the church could and should go in the next several months? Don't be a fire extinguisher; encourage and fuel his holy fire.

Only in church world do we give Debbie Downers a megaphone.

Only in church world do we reap the benefits of a lead pastor's gifting and loudly lament the areas God has not gifted him. By the way, maybe the reason you notice a problem area in your church is because God has gifted and appointed YOU to be the solution!

Criticize by creating. Breathe life, not death, into your church leaders. Nobody likes a Debbie Downer.

EVEN LINCOLN HAD CRITICS

Abraham Lincoln always makes everyone's list of top five presidents ever. He was a courageous leader who walked through hell and saved the Union.

Part of Lincoln's hell was his loud critics. Even guys on his own team took shots. One of his army commanders, George McClellan, described Lincoln (his boss) as "no more than a well-meaning baboon."

In 1863, the *Chicago Times* described one of Lincoln's speeches as "an offensive exhibition of boorishness and vulgarity," adding, "by the side of it, mediocrity is superb."

What was the name of that speech?

The Gettysburg Address.

What's my point? There are no statues of George McClellan or monuments of the *Chicago Times* overlooking the National Mall in Washington. All the great leaders have hecklers.

MAGGOTS IN THE GARAGE

Gripping my piping hot coffee and whisking toward the car parked gingerly in the garage, my senses noticed the first tell-tale sign that something was askew; the sound of rustling—in the garage.

As I approached my car, my eye caught movement on the ground. Was that rice wiggling around? My groggy mind caught up with my senses: MAGGOTS! Something odorous in the flimsy plastic trashcan had attracted, retained, and birthed maggots all because I had missed the trash pick-up two Mondays in a row.

Scratch that. "Missed" isn't the correct term. I hadn't wanted to deal with taking out the trash. Apathy. Laziness. Call it what you want. But I've proven that you reap what you sow.

My failure to deal with the trash (true story!) resulted in writhing maggots, jiggling their pulsating little blobby-bodies like something out of *Star Trek*.

Paul wrote that failing to deal with little pieces of trash in our everyday lives attracts, retains, and births larger spiritual maggots. In Ephesians 4, we wrestle with these words:

> *"Do not let the sun go down on your anger, and give no opportunity to the devil."*

In other words, keep short accounts with people in your life. If something—anything—is rubbing you the wrong way, deal with it immediately.

That day.

Before the sun goes down.

Otherwise that small bit of trash will attract, retain, and birth larger maggots that will jade your perception of reality and eat away at you. Small things quickly become big things if we don't take out the trash right away.

HOW CONAN O'BRIEN DEALT WITH JAY LENO

> "I just want to say to the kids out there watching: You can do anything you want in life. Unless Jay Leno wants to do it too."
> - Conan O'Brien

As we keep short accounts we must strive to share the truth in love. Yes, take care of the trash quickly before it attracts maggots but handle it with grace.

Conan O'Brien was hurt by Jay Leno in 2010. He had been contractually guaranteed the prestigious hosting duties of NBC's *The Tonight Show* six years earlier and within a matter of months of taking on the new gig, he was Leno'd.

Anytime Conan is asked to look back and talk about that painful experience, he adheres to a simple principle: Don't throw the past under the bus, even when you have been Leno'd.

Conan doesn't throw the past under the bus. Even when David Letterman was publicly sniffing for dirty laundry to air on his program (that's what gossips do), Conan did not dishonor NBC.

Leaders don't throw the past under the bus, even when they're Leno'd. There is no honor in tearing down people and organizations ... especially in church world.

Jesus purchased the church with His blood. That's HUGE! God loves the church, created the church, and declares the church to be Christ's bride. Have you ever talked smack about another man's wife? Imagine doing that to Jesus Christ.

If a church has hurt you in the past, that does not give you the right to muddy its name. If a church leader has disappointed you in the past, they are not your enemy (see Ephesians 6:12!). Forgive and let go. The church's role is NOT to dig up dirt on people but to wipe the dirt off people and launch them into their destiny.

Leaders understand that integrity is doing the right thing even when it hurts. Trust me, I've been unjustly hurt many times during my years of ministry. But I've found that God is honored most when we talk smack the least.

If you're a leader who has walked through the fire, allow Isaac's experience in Genesis 26 to be your model. Isaac was misunderstood, dishonored, and shunned over and over again. But he doesn't fight back. He submits to the Lord's will and finds closure in a beautiful display of the gospel:

> *"Isaac asked them, 'Why have you come to me, since you were hostile to me and sent me away?' They answered, 'We saw clearly that the Lord was with you; so we said, 'There ought to be a sworn agreement between us'—between us and you . . . And now you are blessed by the Lord.'"*

I FEEL SORRY FOR CHURCH WORLD CRITICS

In the Book of Nehemiah, we see a man courageously following God's grand vision while enduring great personal criticism and friendly fire. Every pastor and church planter in America walks in Nehemiah's shoes.

I can honestly say that now when I read Nehemiah's story, I'm starting to feel sad for Sanballat and Tobiah. They completely miss out on the miracle. Sanballat and Tobiah mock and jeer, but ache on the inside. After all, only hurting people hurt people.

Jesus said our words and behaviors are simply the overflow of what's already going on in our hearts. If we're at war on the inside, of course we'll be at war on the outside.

Bitterness is the fuel of criticism. Jon Courson once observed, "This is what bitterness does. It's like taking a bottle of poison, swallowing it, and then waiting for the other person to die."

Sanballat and Tobiah are drinking poison, and I genuinely find that sad. It's impossible to build something beautiful with your life when you're swinging a sledgehammer. They need the gospel; a renewed explosion of God's grace in their lives.

Nehemiah is our godly model in being slow to fire back; he predominantly remains gospel-centered and trusts that God will take care of the church critics. He remains faithful to the mission entrusted to him.

And so we pray for those who wish us harm. We out-love, out-serve, and out-bless our critics. We trust God as our guard when we're misunderstood. And we press into these words from Charles Spurgeon:

> "Somebody has said a very nasty thing about us. Well, well; we will answer him when we have got through the work we have at hand, namely, praising God continually. At present we have a great work to do, and cannot come down to wrangle. Self-love and its natural irritations die in the blaze of praise."

HAVE A PLAN

> "Nobody has accomplished anything by believing the naysayers. And few have done so by sticking to proven ideas in proven fields ... If you stop being the scrappy underdog, fighting against the odds, you risk the worst fate of all: mediocrity." - Howard Schultz[16]

I was traveling back from a week-long speaking engagement in Arizona on a flight to Michigan. I sat down, got myself situated for the long flight, and then heard a commotion in the row and seat directly in front.

The seated passenger was talking smack to the flight attendant to the point that he was being loud, obnoxious, and a bit creepy. She left to get the captain and my first thought was, "Holy cow! I'm about to see something go down that will be on the evening news!" I actually hit the HD camera app on my phone and prepared to record whatever UFC match was about to open up.

The captain strolled down the aisle and calmly slid into the seat next to the agitated passenger. In a whispered, soothing tone, he lightheartedly took a few minutes to get to know the passenger and ask him about his life, all of which reduced the tension and calmed the situation.

Long story short, there was no big mid-air take-down or newsworthy ruckus. The captain was a pro; he had a plan ahead of time for how to deal with the situation. He didn't wait for "if." He already had a plan for "when." This eliminated confusion or nerves; he simply had to follow the plan.

You must have a plan for handling your critics ahead of time. You must.

It's a fact. When you sign up for church leadership, you sign up for critics. The only other profession that deals more with Debbie Downers and Chatty Cathies on a regular basis is comedy. Experienced comics plan for hecklers and don't freak out when they appear. They understand it's part of the gig.

You will be criticized. Even Jesus was criticized and had people walk away in a huff (John 6:66). It's time for you to make your plan. Having an automatic default system for dealing with critics will free you from fear and stress.

HOW TO IGNORE LIKE A PRO

> "A man's wisdom gives him patience; it is to his glory to overlook an offense." - Proverbs 19:11

Now, comedians have two choices: ignore or confront. Let's first talk about ignoring a heckler.

When a drunk heckler first starts talking back at the stage, the comic's first instinct is to completely ignore them. If they are just looking to hijack the attention and fail, sometimes they will shut up.

It has taken me years to finally master the art of being Forrest Gump, but once you choose to ignore chronic critics, I can tell you it is freeing. Church leader, I am giving you permission to ignore your critics. I follow these pointers:

- Set-up an email filtering system. Have someone else receive your incoming emails and filter through them for you. It can be a paid staff person or a trusted volunteer. When a negative email arrives from a chronic critic, it automatically gets deleted. You don't need their poison. Trash it.

- Don't respond. Listen to me. Nobody is forcing you to respond to your critics. Even Jesus said not to cast your pearls before swine.

- Don't defend yourself. That's God's deal, not yours. It's the Miranda loophole of critics; anything you say will be used against you.

- Definitely don't surrender your platform to your critics. Critics are arsonists and arsonists only want to burn up your platform.

- Make the delete button your friend. Wear that button out on the keyboard as a badge of honor.

- If something comes via snail mail, you don't have to read it. You don't. Simply write, "Return to Sender." Out of sight, out of mind. And this action sets up a strong boundary to the chronic critic.

- Remember the deep theology of Dr. Seuss. "The people that matter don't mind, and the people that mind don't matter."

HOW TO CONFRONT LIKE A PRO

"Man who catch fly with chopstick accomplish anything."
- Mr. Miyagi

Sometimes a comedian has to outright confront a heckler. It's always awkward and never fun but occasionally necessary for the audience's sake.

When a comic leverages the microphone to shut down a heckler, the aim is to be swift. Pros keep it quick because they want the audience to remain on their side and see the critic as trying to hijack the crowd's enjoyment. If it gets too prolonged, the crowd is apt to take the heckler's side and portray the comic's confrontation through a NATO-like prism—an attack on one is an attack on all.

In ministry, I will absorb any shots that come my way. Anonymous handwritten note? Meet my trash can. Trolling blogger? Delete.

But there is a bright line that, if crossed, will push me to confront . . . taking shots at my family. My role as head of household trumps being pastor of a church. Nobody has the right to take shots at my wife or kids as a way of getting to me. Family is always off limits, and if that line is crossed, then you simply must protect your family.

Please understand that if you must confront, have the mindset of Mr. Miyagi. He was very, very slow to engage but when there were no other options, he swiftly karate chopped those Cobra Kai brats into next week!

In the account of Nehemiah's rebuilding of the wall, he patiently endures and prays.

> "Hear, O our God, for we are despised. Turn back their taunt on their own heads and give them up to be plundered in a land where they are captives." - Nehemiah 4:4 (ESV)

God moves Nehemiah to prepare for confrontation.

> "From that day on, half of my servants worked on construction, and half held the spears, shields, bows, and coats of mail." - Nehemiah 4:16 (ESV)

This deterrent enables the workers to complete their task and rebuild the wall. After the dedication, some more crazy stuff goes down and Nehemiah finally goes all Old Testament on the offenders.

> "And I confronted them and cursed them and beat some of them and pulled out their hair!" - Nehemiah 13:25 (ESV)

The first thing to keep in mind when confronting a heckler: pull out hair, not swords. What I mean is, Nehemiah didn't slay them through the heart with a sword, but he was unapologetically firm. It wasn't a fatal assault, just firm enough to sober them up.

Remember Mr. Miyagi's approach against the leader of the Cobra Kai? He honked his nose in a parking lot. No fatal blows. The aim was to jolt him back to reality and sanity.

Every once in a while, you would even see Jesus confront chronic critics (see Matthew 23, John 8). The aim wasn't to wipe them out, just to point them back to the truth with a swift whack from the Holy Two-by-Four.

Sometimes the hecklers would try to escalate things against Jesus by picking up rocks to throw. This brings us to the second stage of confronting a heckler; prayers, not rocks. You never see godly leaders in the Bible throw rocks; that's an act of the wicked. God does not honor rock throwing (see Acts 7). Instead, the New Testament leaders would pull out the big guns of fervent prayer.

At our church, from day one, I infused our faith community with a DNA of honor and integrity. For us, this means we do not gossip or engage in any insider church politics. We just don't have time—there's a world to be won! When we encounter critics who misunderstand our vision and hearts, we reply by out-loving, out-giving, and out-serving. Occasionally we'll correct if there's a twisting of Scripture (pull out hair, not swords) and always we will pray for those who misunderstand us (prayers, not rocks).

At the end of the day, God has your back if you're following His steps. Don't listen to the bleacher talk; remain focused on the One moving forward.

In the words of John Wesley, "Give me a hundred men who fear nothing but sin and desire nothing but God, and such alone will shake the gates of hell and set up the kingdom of God on earth!"

11

BE YOU

"You are pure potential!" - Martin de Maat

One of the funniest scenes I ever saw live at Second City was during an improv set with Jim Zulevic and Jenna Jolovitz. The couple was sitting on chairs when the audience suggestion was yelled out: "Disney Ride!"

As Jenna sits quietly, Jim begins talking about Disney World's "It's A Small World" attraction, which they are in the midst of riding through. Jim's intricate and detailed knowledge of the inner workings of the animatronics harbors on Disney-stalkerish.

He goes on and on for a few minutes describing in a wry, boring voice about developing this important ride for Disney. The audience begins to nervously laugh not just because of Jim's freakish Wiki-facts he's pulling out of his hat on the spot, but also because of the awkward silence from his scene partner seated next to him.

Finally, Jenna turns to him and yells, "Nobody cares, Jim!"

The audience absolutely erupted in laughter. What contributed to this improvised scene's success was that Jim and Jenna didn't pretend to be someone their not, they acted their age.

Too many young comedians will jump onstage and "become a character." Instead of performing within their age range, actors and actresses will pretend to either be an elderly person or a baby. For some reason, we tend to laugh more easily at people portraying those ages in comedy sketches.

The final *Holy Shift* is easy to remember because it's a phrase many mavericks heard growing up (and if you're reading this book, trust me, you're a maverick). Act your age and be you.

This simple mantra will keep you from getting stuck in your head and always moves the scene along more naturally.

LIFE IS SHORT AND GOD IS BIG

"No matter what people tell you, words and ideas CAN change the world." - Robin Williams

The 2010's have been a time of unique massive tectonic shifts in the world of comedy. That isn't hyperbole, it is fact. On the positive side, 2014 saw the first comedy album to debut at #1 on Billboard since the 1960's (a well-deserved feather in the hat of 'Weird Al' Yankovic).

Particularly during the 2014-2015 season, our culture witnessed the generational baton-passing of several late night torches with the exits of David Letterman, Jay Leno, and Jon Stewart among others. (I still can't believe Arsenio Hall got canceled. That is just wrong.) Jimmy Fallon and Stephen Colbert have ascended to the late night thrones; we have new comedy popes (meaning Jimmy and Stephen just got rare jobs-for-life).

But what struck me most about this time period was the massive loss of comedy giants including Harold Ramis (*Ghostbusters*, *Groundhog Day*, *Stripes*) and Phillip Seymour Hoffman (the guy was funny—have you seen him in Steve Martin's *Leap of Faith*?).

And then, suddenly, in 2014, the world had to grapple with the abrupt loss of Robin Williams.

The news broke during peak social media hours on a Monday evening. Like so many others, I was innocently checking Facebook when I saw post after post of quotes from Dead Poets Society. I turned on CNN and there it was. Robin Williams was gone.

Growing up, I wasn't old enough to appreciate Williams' breakthrough comedy *Mork & Mindy*.

It wasn't until a few years later when I was visiting my grandparents in Burlington, Iowa that I first discovered HBO. You have to understand that in the early 1980s, HBO was relegated to rerunning three movies: *Airplane*, *Spiderman* (the 1970s campy version), and *Popeye*. Over and over these old films would play, and over and over I would slowly absorb the flickering pixels.

Robin Williams was Popeye. I couldn't get enough of him. On a personal note, it is astonishing to me that the same year we lost Williams was the year I lost my grandmother . . . on April Fool's Day, no less.

Anyhow, several years later after Williams kicked his cocaine addiction (he was free-balling with John Belushi on the night of Belushi's overdose, which helped shock Williams toward sobriety), the streak of classic Williams comedies plowed through the culture and onto my teenage radar: *Good Morning Vietnam*, *Hook*, *Mrs. Doubtfire*, *Aladdin*. He was both an improv genius and an acting great.

In 1992, his stand-up career hit its peak on television. Williams was honored to be Johnny Carson's final sit-down interview on *The Tonight Show* the night before Johnny retired. That same month, Williams teamed up with Billy Crystal and Whoopi Goldberg for the fifth installment of *Comic Relief*. The live improv on that particular night had me rolling and I re-watched Williams' on-stage antics over and over again.

Funny enough, it was at church that I was introduced to Robin Williams' finest film: *Dead Poets Society*. I was in confirmation class, that awkward rite-of-passage for all Presbyterian adolescents, and one Sunday our class was allowed to skip the service.

Let me repeat that. Teenagers were being given a pass from the pews. The catch was that we had to sit in the church lounge and watch *Dead Poets Society* (on VHS!).

"Carpe Diem!" raged Williams as teacher John Keating. With wit and passion, we were challenged to leap into life with faith and ferocity. This is one of my favorite quotes from the film:

> "'O Captain, my Captain.' Who knows where that comes from? Anybody? Not a clue?
>
> "It's from a poem by Walt Whitman about Mr. Abraham Lincoln. Now in this class you can either call me Mr. Keating, or if you're slightly more daring, O Captain, my Captain."

Robin Williams made us laugh, yes, but in uncrossing our arms in fits of laughter, he lowered our individual force fields. Once you get a crowd having fun, they will lean in to hear you whisper truths. And Williams did not disappoint through his film roles. The weight and humanity displayed in *Good Will Hunting* and *What Dreams May Come* whispered to us truths about the human condition. I would argue that the latter film, about a husband desperately trying to save his wife from the darkness of deep depression, was as close to an autobiography as we will have of Williams' psyche. How stunning that the disease he fought privately off-stage was a pendulum swing to his on-stage comedic brilliance. It is the twin masks of Comedy and Tragedy.

This is why the loss of Robin Williams blew us all away. There was no warning that we knew of. We were all reminded again that life is short and God is big.

My hope is that as future generations mine his work and life for comedic inspiration, that Williams' final moments of gripping depression would spark us to run toward those who are quietly hurting in our workplaces and neighborhoods today. Shining light on shadows is difficult, but it is our calling. May the loss of Williams not mean the loss of others grappling with very real darkness.

The late Robin Williams had many memorable quotes.

> *"We don't read and write poetry because it's cute. We read and write poetry because we are members of the human race. And the human race is filled with passion. And medicine, law, business, engineering, these are noble pursuits and necessary to sustain life. But poetry, beauty, romance, love, these are what we stay alive for.*
>
> *"To quote from Whitman, 'O me! O life! . . . of the questions of these recurring; of the endless trains of the faithless . . . of cities filled with the foolish; what good amid these, O me, O life?'*
>
> *"Answer. That you are here—that life exists, and identity; that the powerful play goes on and you may contribute a verse. That the powerful play *goes on* and you may contribute a verse. What will your verse be?"*

"Sucking the marrow out of life doesn't mean choking on the bone."

"You're only given a little spark of madness. You mustn't lose it."

"Death is Nature's way of saying, 'Your table's ready.'"

HUMILITY

Remembering the comedy giants who have gone before us reminds us of our own mortality. No matter how well we can make a crowd laugh or how fearless of a leader we may be, life is short. Owning one's mortality makes a person humble. Humility is the mark of a *Comedy-Driven Leader*.

In 1 Peter 5:5, we are told to humble ourselves and serve others. If serving is what a leader does, humility is the fuel of service. Bending a knee and lowering oneself is not an attitude, it is an action.

Indeed, the Scriptures also tell us again in James 4:10 to "humble yourself." Nowhere in the Bible are we told to "be humble." Over and over again, the pathway of leading others involves the action of humility. Many leaders can act humble, but humility is not a feeling or emotion . . . it is something you do.

For example, I can imagine the feelings of running on my NordicTrack. The feelings of excitement over my pace and exhilaration from breaking my own records. But if all I do is think about exercising, at the end of the day, I have done nothing. In fact, if all I do each day is imagine exercising without actually physically doing it, at the end of the month I will discover I'm flabbier and unhealthy.

So it is with humility. *Holy Shift* leaders must actively humble themselves if they are to maximize their organizational influence. Humbling yourself is an exercise:

- When someone cuts you off in traffic, don't flash with rage ... humble yourself.

- If a coworker receives a promotion you deserved ... humble yourself.

- When your teenager acts out in public and embarrasses you ... humble yourself.

The leader who walks in humility is attractive to the follower. Humility helps you keep perspective on what really matters and shapes your heart for compassion toward others.

THE MOST HUMBLE PERSON I'VE EVER KNOWN

Throughout this book, I've shared stories about the late Martin de Maat who was a theater professor at Columbia College in Chicago as well as the Artistic Director of Second City. Martin would always humble himself despite being an accomplished, sought-after improviser.

Martin didn't walk with a swagger but with a limp. His compassion was infectious and it was an honor to have him by my side on my wedding day.

Martin understood the power of humbling yourself, which is remarkable when you count comedy all-stars like Chris Farley and Tina Fey among your students. Being around the movers and shakers of the Chicago comedy-scene always caused Martin to swing his pendulum in the opposite direction; away from power and toward humility. He was always seeking the posture of a student even though he was a wise leader. Martin once shared these words with me about humbling yourself.

> "It is your job to be a student. It is a powerful position. By definition, it is 'one who has yet to know.' It means that the moment you declare yourself a student you clear your slate, need not prove anything, and become pure potential.
>
> "A position of authority contains limitation. Student leaves you wide open to make it up your way. You can improvise your future and the future of the art form. In being its student you are its future."

Often times Martin would be counseling an aspiring comedian or a college student about embracing the here-and-now.

> "Too often we will focus on what's ahead or place ourselves under incredible pressure for just-out-of-reach achievements . . . and that squashes out our humility.
>
> "I do not mean to discourage you or to suggest that it is impossible to make it to 'Mainstage.' Actually being hired in one of the positions we have for actors is highly possible, be it Business Theater or touring company. It is worth the shot if it interests you. What I do want to discourage is your being in 'Level A' wishing you were in 'C,' or being in 'C' in a hurry to be in '1.' This 'where I am is not good enough' pattern is difficult to break. It goes on

and on. You can imagine it as being in a touring company wishing you were in 'etc.,' or 'etc.' wishing for 'Mainstage,' or 'Mainstage' wishing for Saturday Night Live. *Everyone could be busy not doing his or her job. They would be missing much of the present experience while auditioning for the future.*

"Be all right where you are. Commit to the process rather than worrying about the product of your investment. It is the same as improvising. The only way for the next moment to realize its full potential is if 100% of your energy is in this one."

MARTIN'S FINAL WORDS TO YOU AND ME

Humility is being all right where you are. Yes, nurture a holy discontent for what could be and what should be, but nestle your visionary aspirations within a humble heart. Humble confidence is attractive and inspiring to the world.

In the final hours of his life, Martin de Maat dictated one final letter to his students. As we close out this book together, I thought it fitting to share with you Martin's final words to you and me. Glimpsing into the final hours of someone who made a *Holy Shift* helps paint a picture to me of what "success" in life looks like. When you choose to humble yourself as a leader, you are able to share sweet words such as these:

February 13, 2001

I'm dictating this from my hospital bed, so forgive the informality.

Recently my days are filled with doctors. Last Wednesday one of the young interns came in and said, "I have never seen this before." When someone asked what he meant, he said, "I see hundreds of patients, but the people in this room never end, this kind of attention and respect, these visitors, flowers." He paused. "I don't have anything to do with your case, but I feel left out. So if I can answer any questions or help, let me know.

"In the last few weeks the outpouring of support has been wonderful. It is a comfort that cannot be described. I am unimaginably blessed by each of you.

"My primary doctor and close friend returned from a trip to India this week. Imagine him walking into Cabrini's Manhattan Hospital trying to find me. He asked the desk clerk downstairs to find my room number. It is a big place and I have moved. Without pausing, the person behind the desk said, "1124."

"Are you sure?" my friend said, "You didn't even look it up." The desk manager raised her head and replied with a heavy New York accent, "I'm sure. I'm very, very sure. All I say, all day long is 1124."

This room is filled with endless messages, phone calls, stacks of mail and visitors. Please accept this note as thanks. It is important to me that you know that I know how you feel. You mean so much to me. I love each of you and I'm very, very proud of you.

- Martin de Maat, Artistic Director of The Second City

Martin de Maat passed away peacefully surrounded by family and friends on February 15, 2001 at Cabrini Medical Center in New York.

ACKNOWLEDGEMENTS

JESUS—I have a great need for a Savior and a great Savior for my need.

PERRY NOBLE, SCOTT HARRIS, and CHRIS ELROD—You believed in me and cheered for me at a time when I didn't believe in myself. Thank you for speaking Life over my life.

LIFERS —I still can't believe that I get to be your pastor! Your trust and willingness to cannonball into the unknown means the world. I can't wait to see what new adventures lie ahead of us!

MY PARENTS, DAVE and SHARON—Your son is nuts. Thanks for making me this way!

MY KIDS, JOSIAH, AINSLEIGH, and SETH—I love you and I am proud of you. Your dad is nuts.

MY WIFE, AMBER—I love you. You keep me sane.

AND TO MIKE and JASON—Mike, you told me to go write a book. Then you teamed up with Jason to make sure I had time to do just that. And the book I wrote ended up being a bestseller, so thanks for that.

WORKS CITED

1. Jason Zinoman, "Tightrope Comedy, on the Fly," *The New York Times*, July6, 2012. www.nytimes.com/2012/07/06/arts/tightrope-comedy-on-the-fly.html?

2. Interview on Alec Baldwin's podcast, *Here's the Thing*, http://www.wnyc.org/story/197391-kristen-wiig/

3. Augustine of Hippo (as translated by R.P.H. Green), *On Christian Teaching (Book Two)*, (Oxford University Press, 1997).

4. Tina Fey, *Bossypants* (Reagan Arthur Books; 2011).

5. Tina Fey, *Bossypants* (Reagan Arthur Books; 2011).

6. Erwin McManus, *Uprising: A Revolution of the Soul*, Thomas Nelson, 2006.

7. Dave Ramsay, *EntreLeadership: 20 Years of Practical Business Wisdom from the Trenches*, Howard Books, 2011.

8. Tina Fey, *Bossypants* (Reagan Arthur Books; 2011).

9. Mick Napier, *Improvise: Scene from the Inside Out*, Heinemann Drama, 2004

10. Walter Isaacson, *Steve Jobs*, Simon & Schuster, 2011.

11. Scott Raab, "Bill Murray: The ESQ+A," June/July 2012 http://www.esquire.com/entertainment/interviews/a14156/bill-murray-interview-0612/

12. J.B. Philiips, *Letters to Young Churches*, Macmillan, 1960.

13. David Kolinsky, "Scott Adsit on the State of Sitcoms and Why New York Fears the Second City," AVClub.com, December 2009, http://www.avclub.com/article/scott-adsit-on-the-state-of-sitcoms-and-why-new-yo-36145

14. Mick Napier, *Improvise: Scene from the Inside Out*, Heinemann Drama, 2004

15. Donald Miller, "Some Thoughts on Self Promotion and Why Arrogant People Think It's Wrong," March 2012, http://storylineblog.com/2012/03/29/why-i-self-promote/ (accessed March 2012)

16. Howard Schultz, *Pour Your Heart Into It: How Starbucks Built a Company One Cup at a Time*, Hyperion, 1999.

CONTINUE THE CONVERSATION

Resources
FearlessLeaders.net

Blog
JonathanHerron.com

Instagram + Twitter + Facebook
@HighFiveJon

Ministry
LifeChurchMichigan.com

www.ingramcontent.com/pod-product-compliance
Lightning Source LLC
Chambersburg PA
CBHW050317120526
44592CB00014B/1944